ZILLOW
TALK

ZILLOW TALK

THE NEW RULES OF REAL ESTATE

SPENCER RASCOFF AND
STAN HUMPHRIES

GRAND CENTRAL
PUBLISHING

NEW YORK   BOSTON

Photo research and editing by Laura Wyss, Elizabeth Seramur, and Amy Hikida, Wyssphoto, Inc.

Grand Central Publishing
Hachette Book Group
1290 Avenue of the Americas
New York, NY 10104

www.HachetteBookGroup.com

Printed in the United States of America

RRD-C

First Edition: January 2015

10 9 8 7 6 5 4 3 2 1

Grand Central Publishing is a division of Hachette Book Group, Inc.
The Grand Central Publishing name and logo is a trademark of Hachette Book Group, Inc.

The Hachette Speakers Bureau provides a wide range of authors for speaking events. To find out more, go to www.hachettespeakersbureau.com or call (866) 376-6591.

The publisher is not responsible for websites (or their content) that are not owned by the publisher.

Library of Congress Cataloging-in-Publication Data

Humphries, Stan.
    Zillow talk : the new rules of real estate / Spencer Rascoff and Stan Humphries. — First edition.
        pages cm
    Summary: "The CEO and the chief economist of the country's leading real estate web site explain why everything you thought you knew about housing is wrong and how real estate actually works today"— Provided by publisher.
    Includes bibliographical references.
    ISBN 978-1-4555-7474-2 (hardback) — ISBN 978-1-4555-7475-9 (paperback) — ISBN 978-1-4789-7901-2 (audio download) 1. Residential real estate—United States. 2. Real estate business—United States. 3. Real estate investment—United States. 4. Real property—United States. I. Rascoff, Spencer. II. Title.
    HD259.H86 2015
    333.330973—dc23
                                                                    2014024742

To my wife, Nanci, for loving me even as I Zillow-talked her ear off all these years, and to my late brother Justin, whom I miss every day.
—SMR

To my parents, who taught me to be curious and to my wife, who has been game to go where curiosity took me.
—SBH

To all the Zillowites, who have built such an amazing product that a book had to be written about it.
—SMR & SBH

READ THIS BOOK TO FIND OUT WHY...

...it might be better to rent than to buy

...you shouldn't buy the worst house in the best neighborhood

...it's better to remodel your bathroom than your kitchen

...you shouldn't list your house for sale before March Madness or after the Masters

...Starbucks is making some housing markets as frothy as their lattes

...putting the word "cute" in your listing could cost you thousands of dollars

...you should never list your house for $444,000

CONTENTS

MOVING OUT:
THE NEW RULES OF SELLING A HOME

THE DATA-HOOD:
A NEW LOOK AT OUR NATION
OF NEIGHBORHOODS

THIS OLD HOUSING MARKET:
RETHINKING REAL ESTATE IN AMERICA

CONCLUSION

Exterior of the Brady's home from the TV show *The Brady Bunch (ABC/ Photofest)*

Leaving Home

Our Real Estate Journey Begins

THERE ONCE WAS A MAN FROM BENIN

In 1990, when I (Stan) was a Peace Corps volunteer in Benin, an Ohio-sized nation in Sub-Saharan Africa, my housing accommodations were not exactly what you would call luxurious. For a while, I lived in what was essentially a construction site. The house I stayed in had a roof and parts of walls but it clearly was a work in progress. Every time Mr. Sana, the owner, had a few extra dollars, he would buy another batch of bricks and build a little more. By the time I left Benin, the house was mostly finished. The walls literally had gone up around me.

At first, I wondered why Mr. Sana hadn't waited until he could afford enough bricks to build the whole thing at once. But as I got to know more about West African culture, his reasoning finally dawned on me. Like many people in West Africa, Mr. Sana didn't like his cash lying around. That's because, in this society of close-knit families and tribes, people aren't shy about asking for loans and gifts, and local custom makes it very difficult to say no. If Mr. Sana had put his money into a savings account, his family and friends likely would have depleted it. It was safer to convert his cash into bricks and start building, even if he didn't initially have the funds to complete the house.

Homes are certainly an important economic asset but they're

also a highly personal one. Mr. Sana taught me that. Real estate has an emotional dimension that other investments like stocks or mutual funds do not. When you're buying or selling equities, you're guided by financial sensibility, plain and simple. But when you're buying or selling a home, other considerations come into play, like family situations, emotional attachments, and even cultural expectations. Mr. Sana's half-finished walls are the perfect illustration of how unique personal circumstances often shape real estate decisions. And that's equally true in rural Benin and in suburban Seattle.

In 2001, my wife and I moved from Charlottesville, Virginia, to Washington state with our two kids. Since we didn't know the Seattle area very well, the right thing to do would have been to rent for a while and familiarize ourselves with the surrounding neighborhoods before making the commitment to buy. But we had just moved across the country and it was more important for us to have a home of our own—any home—than to have a perfectly located one. Objectively, it wasn't the smartest move, but for our family, at that moment in time, buying a home right away was definitely the way to go.

We looked at almost forty houses in three days. Coming from Virginia, we found Seattle home prices a bit of a shock. At the time, the average home in Seattle was worth $220,000. In Charlottesville, it was just over $150,000.

I remember one house we saw in our price range that didn't even have a front door—you had to enter through the garage. I'd spent years thinking about how cool it would be to take my parents on a tour of my first home. But the thought of showing them a house with no front door, taking them in through the garage, and then telling them the place had cost much more than the home prices they or I were used to just didn't seem right.

So we found another house—this time with a front door. After two years, we sold it at a profit and bought a new one. We were living in that second house in 2008 when the economy tanked and the real estate market plummeted. With home prices crashing around us, I started thinking about how to minimize our own losses. Like

Mr. Sana, we'd converted our money into bricks, and I wanted to protect our investment.

From my perspective as an economist, it seemed like the best move was to sell our house before things got any worse, rent until the market bottomed out, and then purchase our next home at a rock-bottom price. But my wife reminded me that, while selling, renting, and buying again might make good financial sense, it was a pretty terrible idea for our family. By then we had three kids, and uprooting them twice simply wasn't worth it. In our case, the downside of moving far outweighed any potential financial benefits of my scheme to sell, rent, and then buy low. Even during a time of dire economic circumstances, our house was still more than just a financial asset. It was our home.

This all goes to show that real estate decisions are complicated by so many factors that even an economist can't always make them strictly as an economist. That's why, while it may look strange from the outside, building a house brick by brick is sometimes the smartest thing to do for the people on the inside.

Spencer and I wrote *Zillow Talk* to help you figure out the smartest thing to do for the people on the inside of *your* house. This book is about the new rules of real estate. It's intended to help you buy a home or sell a home, and to sound smart when talking about other people buying and selling homes. And it reflects the big bet behind our company, too: Whether you want to spot the *next* hot neighborhood or are deciding whether to buy the worst house in your *current* one, *let the data be your guide.*

SPENCER'S SHADES OF GRAY

Like Stan, I (Spencer) have had my own real estate epiphanies, too—though they took place in Seattle, not Sub-Saharan Africa. Just as Stan learned that walls don't make a home, I learned, a few years back, that it is a rookie error to view a piece of real estate as either for sale or not for sale. In fact, many houses are in a gray area somewhere in between. A homeowner who previously had no intention of selling might suddenly be tempted by a buyer's generous offer. And a homeowner who wants to sell might be persuaded to wait for better market conditions. So if you're willing to operate within those shades of gray, there are a lot of creative ways to end up in the house you want.

When my wife and I moved to Seattle in 2003, we needed somewhere to live, but we weren't quite ready to buy a home. While looking for a house to rent, we came across the perfect place. But there was a catch: The owner wasn't trying to rent it—he wanted to sell it. Since the house had been on the market for about a year, we figured the owner was having trouble finding a buyer willing to pay his asking price, so we wrote him a letter convincing him to rent it to us instead. (All we knew was the house's address. We had to send the letter by snail mail.) The alternative for the homeowner was selling at a loss or continuing to pay the mortgage out of his own pocket. Renting to us was therefore a win-win for us all, we suggested. Luckily for us, he agreed. He took the "For Sale" sign out of the yard, and we moved in.

We were still renting that house two years later when we learned that my wife was pregnant with our first child. There's some social pressure to buy a house when you're starting a family. (Plus, Zillow was just getting off the ground, and it dawned on me that an executive of an online real estate company should probably own his own home.) Then again, we were happy in our rented home. So we called up our landlord and made him an offer to buy the home we were renting. It couldn't have worked out better. Even though our offer was below market value, the owner ended up doing fine. He got more for the house than he would have if he'd sold it in 2003, *plus* he'd collected thirty-six months of rent from us. Also, by selling the house to the rental tenant, he didn't miss a single month of rent. Meanwhile, my wife and I purchased the home we already loved at a very favorable price.

If we'd let the "For Sale" sign on that house scare us away when we were looking to rent, we would have missed out on a really great opportunity. Instead, our first successful real estate adventure expanded our sense of what's possible and encouraged us to keep exploring that gray area between for sale and not for sale. Since then, we've continued to buy and sell through somewhat unconventional methods.

After our second child was born in 2008, we decided to look for a bigger house. It was time for our family to move, but it was a horrible time to sell, given the state of the housing market. So we did exactly what the previous owner had done: We found a couple that wanted to rent the house with the option of eventually buying it later. In fact, we agreed to set some of their rent money aside each month in a down-payment fund.

Although the market was already pretty bad, we expected it was going to get even worse, and we didn't want to buy before it bottomed out. So, in the meantime, we moved into a rental and watched real estate prices continue to fall. In early 2012, Stan's analysis revealed that the real estate market had hit bottom in our area, and we decided to pursue a house that looked promising: a high-end foreclosure.

The previous owner had bought the home in 2005, at the height of the market, and put considerable work into the property before times got tough and the bank foreclosed. By the time we had the title and keys, it had fallen into total disrepair (as we discuss elsewhere, this is common with foreclosures). But even so, we got a great deal: We ended up paying a little more than *half* of what the seller originally paid for it—plus we got a 3 percent mortgage. One year and several contractors later, our home was worth nearly twice what we'd paid for it.

As this book goes to press, my wife and I are looking for an investment property that can double as a vacation home, and the one we have our eye on is in yet another unconventional transaction: a short sale. As it turns out, buying a short sale can be pretty complicated. Even though there's a "For Sale" sign in the yard, once again, the situation is hardly black and white. The home we're hoping to purchase is owned by *seven* different lenders, which means we have to negotiate with all of them at once. It feels like every time we move closer to a resolution, we take two steps back. On the spectrum of for sale to not for sale, this house is its very own shade of gray.

In our own ways, and from our own respective journeys with homeownership, Stan and I have learned something really fundamental: Real estate is a lens on society. What we're hoping to do with this book, then, is three-fold:

We want to use Zillow's data to get you to rethink how you buy, sell, finance, and live in your home.

We want to use it to revisit and revise some tired old myths—for instance, whether homeownership really should be inseparable from the American Dream, and whether the sacred Mortgage Interest Deduction actually does more harm than good to our economy.

And, finally, we want to show exactly how—and how much—the rules of real estate have changed in our fast-paced, hyper-connected, smart phone–wielding world.

LOOK OUT, HERE COMES A FOUNDATION MYTH

I (Spencer) actually came to the world of real estate quite by accident. In fact, I was much more interested in harnessing the power of technology to dis-intermediate—as the parlance goes—a completely different industry: the travel industry.

For years, it may well have been your worst nightmare: not snakes, not public speaking, not heights—which, according to Gallup, are Americans' three top fears.[1] No, I'm talking about booking the family vacation—an experience that, as recently as the early 1990s, involved dialing, say, Great West Airlines, being made to wait on hold, and listening to not-so-soothing Muzak, all while muttering, or begging, or screaming to talk to a human being.

When you finally got through, you would ask if such-and-such a flight was available on a particular day. You would hear the clicking of computer keys on the other end. You would wait some more. And then you would get your answer: "Sorry, but we don't have a flight from here to there."

Such was the state of the American travel industry during the pre-Internet age. Consumers had little to no control over getting where they wanted, staying where they needed, or seeing exactly which ticket, car, or hotel was more or less expensive than the next. The information that could have helped them plan a family vacation with ease was locked up in secret databases. Only industry insiders could get their hands on the keys.

I knew I needed to get my hands on those keys, and I was willing to bet that many other people felt likewise. That's how I came to co-found Hotwire, the discount travel website, in 1999. The idea was simple: If everyone could simply jump through the phone, peer at the travel agent's screen, and see the flight and fare information for him or herself, we'd all be better off. And, indeed, several years later, consumers *were* better off. The travel industry had been transformed, thanks in part to Hotwire, and also to sites like Expedia, which acquired Hotwire in 2003—a serendipitous event in Stan's and my lives because, at the time, Stan was working at Expedia.

Stan was in charge of the Expedia team that was exploring creative ways to use data. When we first met, we realized that we had a pretty strong, shared interest in that topic. We both were thrilled about the possibilities of bending data to empower ordinary people during the heyday of the online revolution. The rest, as they say, is history.

During that same time period, of course, other business innovators were using the fledgling World Wide Web to bring similar transparency to a host of formerly opaque, anti-consumer, or consumer-unfriendly industries. For the first time, people could research and buy stocks, cars, and insurance policies online—to say nothing of music (a story for another day).

Nevertheless, six years into the twenty-first century, at least one major American industry had yet to be transformed by easy access to online information. And this was not just any industry, mind you, but one of the very largest and most important: the United States' $1.2 *trillion* real estate marketplace.

It's shocking to think back and consider that, before Zillow started in 2006, in order to shop for a home, you had to scour the real estate listings in the local Sunday newspaper. Some real estate information had been computerized, but much of it was only available to real estate professionals. Even so, those early, exclusive computer files only contained part of the historical information readily available today, including past sale prices and assessed values.

In other words, the information ordinary people wanted and needed to know was guarded in county courthouses and secret industry databases. Practically speaking, it was nearly impossible to learn online what the home down the street sold for, how the tax assessor had most recently valued it, or what it was likely to be worth on the local market.

Shopping for a home was like being in a dark room where only the agent was holding a flashlight. She'd shine it on two or three homes—listings or "comps" she had chosen for you—but all you wanted to do was grab the flashlight and wield it yourself. Or, better still, just flip on the darned light switch to see it all.

That's why we created Zillow: to turn on the lights and bring transparency to one of our country's largest and most opaque industries. So on February 8, 2006, a new website with a funny name launched to the world, with the power to estimate—or, as we call it, "Zestimate"—the value of nearly every home in America.

Within hours, hundreds of thousands of people flocked to the site. A new verb was born, as home after home was "Zillowed," and we discovered that there were a lot of people out there who shared our curiosity, our envy, and our voyeurism.

One million people visited Zillow.com in its first three days of operation, crashing our wee little servers in the process. Soon "Zillow" and "Zestimate" became part of the zernacular (I mean vernacular). The business of owning or shopping for a home was forever changed, and we no longer had to answer the question, "What do you do for a living?" with some lengthy explanation involving metaphors and hand gestures. We had become, as CNBC's *Mad Money*'s Jim Cramer put it in 2014, "the keeper of the numbers."

Today, Zillow is the largest real estate site on the Web and on mobile, with 90 million people (unique users) visiting Zillow and its associated mobile apps every month. With data and information on more than 110 million homes—including Zestimates, homes for sale, homes for rent, hundreds of thousands of real estate agent reviews, and other useful information—homeowners, home shoppers, and curious neighbors rely on Zillow for "inside" information not found anywhere else.

Of course, the real power that Zillow provides to consumers doesn't come from all this data alone—it comes from our analytics. We built Zillow by first amalgamating all the information on housing we could possibly get our hands on. At first, that meant turning to public records that contained information like a home's number of bedrooms and bathrooms, taxes, and square footage. We took all that data and used it to calculate the value—the Zestimate—of nearly every single home in America. We even went through a similar process to create "Rent Zestimates" for homes all across the United States, estimating what a particular home could reasonably be expected to rent for.

Before long, we took the Zestimate a step further and began to forecast it. In the end, we wound up with a method that could estimate and predict the value of virtually every home in America.

People now have access to all the information they need in one place, and the analysis to translate this data into usable information. But we also think the democratization of real estate data is profoundly important. It's been said that the enemy of truth isn't the lie, but the myth. Well, this book is all about deploying the data to replace folklore with facts.

As you'll see, the numbers tell us that homeownership *isn't* the right choice for everyone. A remodeled kitchen *doesn't* give you the biggest bang for your home improvement–project buck. A well-timed listing will do far *more* for your sale price than freshly baked cookies at an open house ever could. And that, with apologies to twentieth-century British property baron Lord Harold Samuel (who purportedly coined the phrase "there are three things that matter in property: location, location, location,") the three things that matter in property are *future location*, *future location*, *future location*.[2]

OUR FLOOR PLANS, OURSELVES

The data also shows us how much the market has changed in the past half-century—both in terms of our physical experience of the home and its overall importance in our lives and our economy.

In 1950, the average number of residential square feet per person in the United States was less than 300. By 2000, that figure had climbed to almost 900—both because homes got a lot bigger and families got a bit smaller.[3]

But that's only half the story. During essentially that same time frame, this same trend reversed in the workplace. In 1970, companies used to plan an average of 600 square feet per employee when designing industrial and commercial facilities. Today, thanks to improved technology, a devotion to collaboration, and the near-extinction of office libraries, secretaries, and "computer rooms," the average number of square feet per person in an office has shrunk to less than 100. In other words, if the American home-to-work space ratio used be something like 1:3, today it is 7:1. In still other words, there has been a more than twenty-fold increase in the significance of our homes in our day-to-day lives.

In turn, the home itself has changed radically as a result. In 1970, the word "telecommuting" had not been invented, workout rooms consisted of a tricked-out piece of elastic tied to your doorknob, and it was unheard of to have anything in your house akin to a movie theater. Today, according to the National Association of Home Builders, an exercise room is one of the top ten features that "Home Buyers Really Want" in an upscale home. A media room is almost as desirable. More than 34 million people work from home at least occasionally.

Our homes are not merely bigger and more versatile these days; they also embody the privatization of a whole host of activities that used to be exclusively commercial—from the gym, to the movies, to coffee shops, to the workplace itself. And, yes, Robert Putnam, we even *bowl* at home—on our TVs and in our living rooms, thanks to the magic of Wii and Xbox.

The upshot is that our homes are now much more than the places where we lay our heads at night. And they aren't just "where the heart is" anymore, either. Homes are the object of our heart's desire.

We now fantasize about upsizing our houses by viewing "real estate porn" online and on dozens of home-related TV shows—spending massive hours on shows like *American Dream Builders*, *Extreme Makeover Home Edition*, *House Hunters*, and the *Million Dollar Listing* franchise. Not to mention snooping on Zillow to find home information, sale prices, and even pictures of the homes of our bosses, colleagues, prospective dates, ex-girlfriends, aging parents, and ex-girlfriends' aging parents.

There's no question that our culture is real estate–obsessed. But there's a difference between fixation and comprehension. And in our view, housing is the most important industry in America that almost nobody understands. Housing is Issue #1 in the Oval Office, in the corner office, and at the kitchen table.

Yet, even though it's at the top of mind for everyone from celebrities to central bankers, real estate is far from a perfect market. Up until very recently, home buyers and sellers essentially met in the dark to shake hands on the basis of hunches and guesses. National policy makers advanced gut-level theories about the nexus between homeownership and individual and community well-being. Capital markets placed trillion-dollar bets on real estate trends, based on little more information than what's available to the average home buyer, and then watched as their investments plummeted and took the global financial system with them.

How can the real estate market—a market that is both so personally intimate and macro-economically consequential—be such a complete mystery?

A few observations:

First, the data on housing simply hasn't been widely available. Before Zillow, as we mentioned, the few real estate databases that existed were primarily kept in leather-bound volumes on the endless shelves of county office buildings or in privately held industry databases inaccessible to the rest of us.

Second, and perhaps more importantly, *we were afraid to ask.* Widespread homeownership seemed like such an unmitigated virtue that no one wanted to dig too deeply. When the slot machine keeps paying out, why raise a hand to ask if it might be broken?

Moreover, sunlight isn't just the best disinfectant. It exposes us, too. Because so many Americans are homeowners, we didn't necessarily want the real estate market to suffer the same price reductions (or are they "corrections"?) that upended the car, stock, insurance, and travel markets. Quite the contrary, far too many of us wanted—and expected—our home values to continue rising, year after year.

The good news is, the era of ignorant bliss is demonstrably, definitively over. Everybody understands that housing bubbles can pop. And we all want better, more accurate information to prevent bubbles from inflating in the first place.

A BETTER HOUSE TRAP

A decade or so ago, if you wanted an estimate of your home's value, it took several hours (after weeks of waiting), a trained professional appraiser (who was rarely free when you were), and at least nine hundred dollars. Today, Zillow can estimate a home's value instantaneously, using tools more familiar in genomics, image compression, and biochemistry than pencils, measuring tapes, and Polaroid cameras. Although Zillow will never replace appraisers, it gives homeowners, investors, and policy makers another tool to use in understanding a home's potential value. And, most importantly, it does so without human limitations. Creating valuations for every home in America is extremely complicated. Think about the scale on which we're working. Hundreds of thousands of lines of code. Dozens of servers. More than a million unique valuation models. All told, our computers process 3.2 terabytes of data every day.

Just to give you a sense of the investment on our end: We're constantly reevaluating and revising our algorithms. These algorithms are created by teams of experts with PhDs. In the past several years alone, we've gone from a 13.6 percent margin of error to a less than 7 percent margin of error, while increasing Zestimate coverage from 43 million to more than 100 million homes.

Our multiple databases—all of which are living, breathing, and improving every single day—are central to the genesis of this book. Thanks to newly accessible data and the ability to mine it, we deconstruct some of the falsehoods that have clouded important facts about the housing market, and we reveal data-driven truths that can help all of us—buyers, sellers, observers, analysts, and legislators—to make better decisions going forward.

We talk about some of the most interesting trends and patterns that we've seen, and we describe their implications.

Sometimes, that means busting myths. Other times, it means affirming them—with a few, slight modifications. (*Do property values rise the closer you are to a Starbucks?*)

Sometimes, we turn conventional wisdom on its head. Other times, we explain why conventional wisdom may be right, but for the wrong reasons. (*What neighborhood is most likely to gentrify next?*)

We tell sellers when and how to list—and we tell buyers why they might want to interpret those listings in ways they hadn't imagined. (*What's an easy way to spot desperation in a seller?*)

We explain when a potential buyer in a particular place is most likely to look for a new home. And we reveal when peak interest and short supply coincide to create the perfect sellers' market. (*What does your street suffix say about the age of your home?*)

We also shed light on why America needs to rethink some of its old dogmas about real estate and housing—from the mortgage interest deduction to flood insurance.

Our goal in this book is to ARM (bad mortgage pun intended) you with new tools—and to help you navigate the vastly changed real estate market that we find ourselves in post-recession. And, equipped with our data and analysis, we hope to help you pair your passion for homes with information that will empower you with new rules to make smart decisions about where to live, how to sell, what to buy, and how Washington can facilitate a healthier housing market.

After all, this is why we created Zillow—to marry our left-brain obsession with data and our right-brain love affair with homes; to create a new force for transparency in an industry that seemingly everyone cares about, but virtually no one fully understands.

The name Zillow is a hybrid of "zillions" and "pillows"—what English majors call a portmanteau. Zillions represents the analytical, quantitative side of who we are—the zillions of data points and calculations we crunch to help better understand the housing market. Pillows, where we lay our heads at the end of the day, are an iconic representation of the emotional importance that homes have in our lives.

Ultimately, we want to help you make sense of the zillions so you can rest more easily.

At Zillow, we know that a house is more than an address on a street, or a place you keep your stuff. Home is where your life happens. And here, in this book—just like on our website and across our apps—our aspiration is actually pretty simple: helping you find your way home.

THE ZESTIMATE: WHAT'S MY HOME *REALLY* WORTH?

It's the oldest question in real estate, yet up until recently it was nearly impossible to quickly get an estimate for free. Well into the 1990s, the best option was looking at the recent sale prices of surrounding homes (or what real estate professionals call "comps," short for "comparable sales"), guesstimating a rough value per square foot, and then applying that to your own home. But that method was lacking, to say the least, compared to the free estimates widely available today.

By the time Zillow came onto the scene in 2006, computers and statistical models had updated the process. In those days, a statistician often would handcraft a complicated model to calculate home values. This was a huge improvement over the comp and guesstimate method. It also was a time-consuming, painstaking process, because the statistician would have to plug an enormous number of variables into his or her model—everything from a house's number of bathrooms to its proximity to the local dump. Virtually everything that could affect the price had to be taken into account.

This kind of value estimation also came with big drawbacks. For one thing, these models really only worked over fairly large geographic areas. With a statistician hand-programming the model, it simply wasn't practical to refine different versions of the model and then to apply them to each and every neighborhood in the country. So it was rare to have a model that zeroed in much closer than the state or metro level.

Imagine using the same model to calculate the value of homes in celebrity-studded Miami and the panhandle on the other side of the state. See the problem?

When we founded Zillow, we were determined to build a better home value estimate—one that truly incorporated all of the idiosyncrasies that determine a home's value. So in 2005, we got to work.

First, we scoured the research—and we didn't stop with techniques specific to real estate. We borrowed from those more commonly used in fields like artificial intelligence, biogenetics, genomic research, and image processing, among others. These methods might have been designed for problems like marking cancer cells or making fuzzy images clearer, but we found that they could be applied to make home values clearer as well.

Right away, we discovered something significant: It turned out that those gigantic, complex models really weren't the best approach. Instead, we found that we could actually get much more accurate data by deploying a lot of relatively simple models.

To understand why, imagine two photographers who want to capture the image of a house. One spends hours positioning his camera, waiting for just the right light, and then snaps a photo. The other walks around the house taking a whole bunch of pictures—even climbs a ladder to photograph the roof—and then uses a computer program to combine those photos into a 3D image of the home. If you wanted to learn the most about the house, which image would *you* turn to?

In the same way, we're able to account for almost every angle of a home's value by using hundreds of simple models. They factor in a home's lot size, its number of bedrooms, and virtually all of the elements that might affect home value. And because these models are much smaller, they're able to weigh all of those variables based on hyper-local history. Instead of treating entire states like homogenous markets, these smaller models are able to account for the value differences that occur from street to street.

Most importantly, our models refine and retrain themselves nightly. Every single night, our computers build about 1.2 million statistical models, which immediately start calculating home values in every corner of the country. Once they've finished the job, those models are deleted. The next night, another 1.2 million models are built based on the new conditions of a brand-new day, and the process repeats.

Because of this constant refinement, our home value estimates catch any changing conditions that might affect home values as soon as they shift. That's how we get the Zestimate—the most accurate, up-to-date home valuations we are able to create.

STEALING HOME

HOME

SCORING A DATA-DRIVEN DEAL
ON A NEW HOUSE

Highclere Castle, located in Hampshire, England, is the home of the Crawley family in *Downton Abbey (Stan Humphries)*

Warren Buffett Is (Always) Right

Why Buying a Home Is Still a Really Smart Investment

It's hard to think of an investor with more credibility than the "Oracle of Omaha," Warren Buffett. From his perch atop the central plains, Buffett sees all. And, as the longtime chairman of Berkshire Hathaway, the massive holding company, Buffett nearly *owns* all, too. If you want a single measure of Buffett's success as an investor—aside from the fact that, at the moment, he's the third richest person on Earth[1]—here it is: From 1964, when Buffett began gobbling up businesses, through 2012, the value of Berkshire's stock has soared 586,817 percent.[2] Today, Berkshire's holdings include dozens of famously successful companies, from GEICO to Brooks Running to American Express. The result is that a dollar invested in Berkshire in 1964 is worth more than $500,000 today.

Enough said. The guy knows investing.

Every year, Buffett grants a lengthy "Ask Warren" interview to CNBC's *Squawk Box*, during which the show's anchors ask every conceivable question about his investment strategies, economic forecasts, the weather in Nebraska...you name it. And, because Buffett is the undisputed master of the markets, people listen carefully to what he has to say. Very carefully.

During Buffett's inquest in February 2012, our ears perked up when CNBC's Becky Quick, the co-host, asked Buffett, "Do you still think that this is a great time to be buying stocks?" "Yes," he replied, right before he changed the subject from equities to real estate. But "if I had a way of buying a couple hundred thousand single-family homes," he said, "...I would load up on them."[3]

Quick then asked whether Buffett would advise young investors to put their money in stocks, or use their savings to buy a first home. Buffett replied that buying a home with a thirty-year mortgage, at the historically low interest rates of early 2012, was "a terrific deal" and "as attractive an investment as you can make now."[4]

For obvious reasons, we were very happy to hear Buffett encourage people to shop for homes. And Buffett didn't just speak. He acted. Berkshire Hathaway has recently purchased more than a dozen real estate brokerages, and during 2013, Buffet launched his own: Berkshire Hathaway HomeServices. It's safe to say that the Oracle is putting his money where his mouth is.

But let's suppose you're not a billionaire investor. If you're in the market for just one house, instead of a few hundred thousand, does Buffett's advice still apply? Should you invest in real estate? Are single-family homes really a better deal than stocks?

Most people think so. Even in our post–housing bubble world, Americans have held fast to the belief that real estate is always a surefire way—and usually the very best way—to grow your money. A 2011 Pew Research Center survey found that 81 percent of adults in the United States believe that "buying a home is the best long-term investment a person can make."[5] Each month, Fannie Mae tracks consumer sentiment about the housing market specifically, and the economy more generally. The response to one question in particular has remained remarkably steady over the past several tumultuous years: When potential movers are asked whether they would rather rent or buy, two out of every three have consistently told Fannie that they would rather buy.[6] In other words, as the housing market was continuing to bottom-out, and as foreclosures were still on the rise, the public's confidence in residential real estate was—and remains—incredibly high.

To see if that confidence was warranted, we decided to crunch the data. And there's an awful lot of it to crunch.

According to the World Bank, the US stock market is worth more than $18.7 trillion.[7] Just to put that number in perspective, it's a few trillion dollars more than the entire annual gross domestic product of the United States. If you can believe it, though, the housing market is even bigger. According to recent estimates, the value of America's housing stock is more than $25.7 trillion.

Furthermore, in addition to being really big, both the US housing and equities markets are very old. That means we have access to a huge volume of data over a longtime horizon—an economist's dream come true! (No really, this is what Stan dreams about at night.)

When we compare these massive markets, at first blush, stocks seem to easily outperform real estate. From 1970 to 2010, the Standard & Poor's (S&P) 500—an index that is widely accepted to reflect the overall performance of the stock market—showed an annualized increase in price of between 8 and 11 percent. Home prices, on the other hand, rose an average of 4 percent per year during that same span.

On its face, then, the better investment looks like the stock market, hands down.

But in order to truly evaluate their relative performance, we need to make this an apples-to-apples comparison. Obviously, there are financial benefits to holding stocks and owning real estate that aren't reflected in their paper value. When you own stocks, for instance, you often earn dividends as a shareholder. When you own a house, on the other hand, you're building equity and lessening your tax burden, thanks to a few lines in the US tax code that allow homeowners to write off the interest on their mortgages (more on this in Chapter 25).

Oh yeah, and try living in a stock, or renting it out on Airbnb.

Real estate does triple duty as somewhere to put your money, your stuff, and yourself...or your tenants.

We won't bore you with the math, but when factoring all of these variables and distinctions into our calculations—from stock dividends, to rental income, to tax advantages—the result surprised even a couple of die-hard real estate fans like us. Based on our analysis, from 1975 to 2014, the S&P 500 averaged an annual return of 10.4 percent, while residential real estate returned 11.6 percent each year on average. That's right: All things being equal, investing in real estate is definitely the better bet.

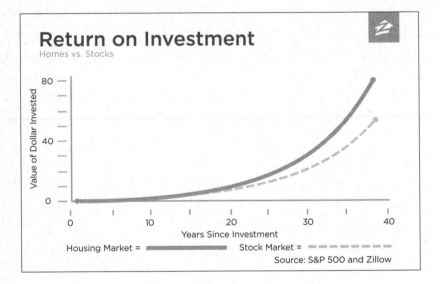

Historically speaking, and accounting for all of the important distinctions between real estate and stocks, real estate wins the day—though only by 1.2 percent. Still, as the graph above illustrates, over the long haul, even a small difference in the average return on investment can result in a very big payoff, because returns are compounded each and every year. That's why, beyond the twenty-year mark, the solid line (real estate) races above and beyond the dotted line (stocks).

Meanwhile, there's another reason that real estate beats stocks as a long-term investment: volatility. Investing in the stock market is often compared to riding a roller coaster, and for good reason. The value of a stock (or an entire portfolio, for that matter) can sky-rocket or nose-dive over the course of any given year, month, day, or even hour. These peaks and valleys are especially bumpy—in other words, risky—over short periods of time. Over long periods of time, investing in the stock market is less risky, to be sure. But historically, whatever the time frame—a year, a decade, or longer—housing is always less volatile than stocks, as you can plainly see in the graph below.

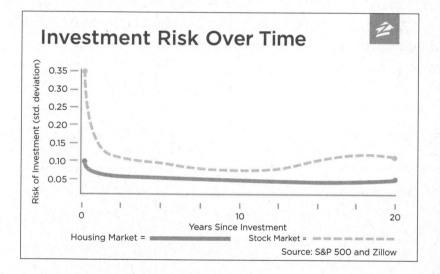

Investing in real estate also beats investing in the stock market in a final way that's worth noting, and that's not reflected in our analysis above. As we explore at length elsewhere in this book, the majority of Americans take out a mortgage to purchase real estate. That is, they leverage a down payment of 10, 20, or 30 percent to secure a loan for the full cost of their investment. If you have $100,000 to invest in real estate, by taking out a mortgage, you can buy a $500,000 house. On the other hand, if you invest $100,000 in the stock market, you end up with $100,000 in stocks (or even a bit less, after brokers' fees). Technically, it's possible to leverage your investment in the stock market as well (it's called "buying on margin"), but the process is tricky, and not generally available to the average retail investor.

We would never suggest that real estate is the bulletproof investment it seemed to be ten or twenty years ago. Things have changed. This much we know.

What hasn't changed, despite the crash of the housing market and the slow economic recovery, is that residential real estate is still a terrific place to put your savings. The returns are better than stocks. The risks are lower. And the benefits—from tax write-offs, to leverage, to a roof over your head—are more significant, too.

We suppose it's no surprise that Warren Buffett was right. His advice, after all, is always on the money.

Exterior of Carrie Bradshaw's brownstone apartment from the TV show *Sex in the City* (Photofest)

2

Stats and the City

Timing Is Everything When Deciding Whether to Buy or Rent

On April 23, 2012, HBO's *Sex and the City* became home-less.[1] The brownstone exterior and steps where much of the show was filmed—home to so many of Carrie Bradshaw's mishaps and musings—was taken, like Carrie herself, off the market.

Off-screen, of course, the home isn't the cozy, one-bedroom flat on the Upper East Side that was seen on TV. It's actually a sprawling, five-bedroom town house in the West Village. It boasts 12-foot ceilings, marble fireplaces, and a sunroom. And when, in reality, New York's most famous fictionally rent-controlled brownstone sold, it went for an eye-popping $13.2 million.[2]

This vast disparity between fact and fiction did not go unnoticed. "As a freelance journalist in one of the most expensive cities to live in," one blogger noted, "Carrie Bradshaw would never have been able to afford such expansive digs."[3] No doubt, the character who confessed to buying *Vogue* instead of dinner when she first moved to New York would agree.

But there's a reason that Sarah Jessica Parker's character found herself in a rented apartment that was, for all intents and purposes, a yuppie paradise. It's the same reason that we never saw moving trucks pull up to the white picket fences of the Bradys, the Cleavers, or the Dunphys of ABC's hit sitcom *Modern Family*. In Hollywood's eyes, young professionals—from *Friends* to *Seinfeld*—should rent, while happy families in the 'burbs ought to own.

This notion has been seared into the public consciousness, sometimes without us even realizing it. There are certain points in life when we all feel, instinctively, that we're supposed to rent. And there are certain points when we're overcome by the almost primal urge to buy. But how do we know when the time is really right?

We take our cues from the expectations of our family and friends, from popular culture, and from our gut—or whatever it is that makes our heart race when we see our dream house. In fact, for many people, the idea of owning a home is not a choice—it's a progression. It's how you know that "real life" has begun.

But that's *Sex and the City*, not "Stats and the City." The truth is, our thinking about homeownership is rooted mostly in sentiment—not statistics.

THE BREAKEVEN HORIZON

When the two of us looked at the data, we got a more nuanced idea of the virtues of buying versus renting. In fact, we were able to construct something that we call the "breakeven horizon" for every area in the country. What that number tells us is that sometimes a single, working woman in the big city is better off buying. And believe it or not, a picture-perfect suburban family may find that it makes better financial sense to rent.

To show you what we mean, let's consider two families living in two very different circumstances.

The Smiths are a young, engaged couple living in Washington, DC. They were college sweethearts at Brown University, and now John is a successful freelance writer, while Laura works at a non-profit organization. They're both huge foodies, appreciate a good music scene, and chose to move to Washington's trendy U Street neighborhood.

John and Laura are classic renters, right?

Then there are the Joneses, Tom and Terri. Tom served in the

Army during the First Gulf War, and now works as a high school history teacher. They lived in San Jose, California, until recently, when Tom's wife, Terri, who works in corporate finance, was transferred to a branch of her company in New Castle County, Delaware. The Joneses have two children—Matt and Marie—ages eleven and fourteen, respectively. The Joneses have taken a liking to the upscale suburb of Greenville, Delaware, just a short drive from Terri's office, and a choice location for commuters to Wilmington and Philadelphia. Now they're debating whether to rent or buy a house. Prices are high, just like in San Jose, and with a couple of kids, buying a place seems like it would make sense.

Historically, the Smiths and the Joneses would have had to rely on what are called price-to-rent ratios, which compare the average sale price of homes in an area to average annual rents there. If the ratio were low—a typical rule of thumb is less than 15—they'd probably decide to buy. If it were high, they'd likely opt for a rental.

But price-to-rent ratios fall short for three somewhat technical reasons. First, they compare very different types of housing stock. Second, they ignore the significant transaction costs (and somewhat offsetting benefits) of buying. And third—most importantly for the Smiths and Joneses—they're not particularly helpful to regular people. For an economist? Interesting. For a nervous, first-time buyer? Confusing.

That's why, frustrated with the unscientific ways people assess buying versus renting, we zeroed in on the one factor that we think is both fundamental and grossly overlooked: *how long you plan to live in a home.*

Intuitively, everyone understands that you should rent if you're only living somewhere for one year—but that renting for 20 years is probably not cost-effective. What the *breakeven horizon* does is figure out where those two paths cross to pinpoint the number of years it would take to make buying economically preferable to renting the same home. Then you just have to decide how long you're likely to stay. If it's longer than the breakeven horizon, buy. If it's not, rent.

For any given home, the breakeven horizon conveniently compares renting versus buying by taking into account the *full* net costs of both—including down payments, closing costs, mortgage payments, property taxes, utility costs, maintenance costs, tax benefits, and even home value and rent appreciation. We make the calculation even more meaningful by using Zillow's forecast of home values in the area. Once we take all that data into account, our equation produces the number of years after which the *real* costs of buying become less than or equal to the *real* costs of renting. In other words, the breakeven horizon addresses all the problems of existing metrics by converting the relevant information into a single number that actually means something to home shoppers.

For instance, here are the relative breakeven horizons from the first quarter of 2014 for a handful of major metro areas. As you can see, they vary significantly.

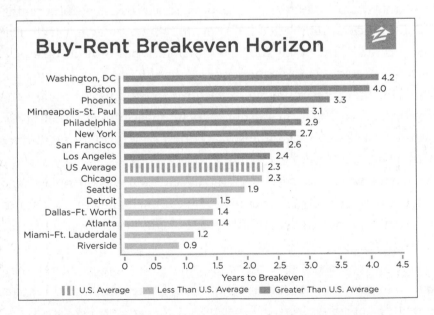

This chart shows how long a person must plan to live in their home before it makes financial sense to buy the home instead of renting the same property. For example, if you live in New York and you're planning to spend more than 2.7 years in your home, you'd be better off buying than renting the home.

So returning to the Smiths and the Joneses—who are anxiously tapping their feet in their agents' offices—all we have to know is how long they plan to stay in their respective homes. Sure, in these wildly unpredictable times, that may be tough to say for certain. But your best guess of how long you plan to live in one property is probably a lot better than one-size-fits-all advice from rankings that have never met you.

John and Laura love DC. They're happy with their jobs. And, in their neighborhood, it turns out that it's cheaper for them to buy if they plan to live in their home just over five years. Even if they do move 5.6 years from now, buying is still the better move.

Surprisingly, in 267 out of 339 metros—nearly 80 percent—the breakeven horizon is less than three years, meaning owning a home is often smarter than we might otherwise think. Of course, a big part of the currently low breakeven horizon in many metros is the enormous reset in home prices that occurred during the housing recession and the extraordinarily low mortgage rates.

For Tom and Terri, though, the situation is a little different. Before, when they lived in San Jose and planned on staying there, it didn't take Big Data to determine that buying there made sense. But living in Greenville, the breakeven horizon is a lengthy 8.4 years. That is, as a purely economic matter, buying won't be worth it unless they stay almost nine years—more than two times longer than the average employee sticks around. Matt and Marie will both be off to college, and out of the house, by then. So even though we tend to think that owning a home is always the right thing when you have kids, finding a nice rental may be the better option for the Joneses.

If the Joneses choose to rent, it just means that they won't end up living in a house that's bigger than they need after the kids go to college. Instead of paying high property taxes, mortgage payments, and other costs of homeownership, they'll have the flexibility to move if they so desire.

Sometimes renting gets a bad reputation in our society. It's associated—rightly or wrongly—with transience, youth, and folks who haven't started their "real lives" yet. This idea permeates popular culture. Carrie Bradshaw, the trendy but unsettled heroine, is a renter; Claire Dunphy, the got-it-together mom on *Modern Family*, is an owner. But as Tom and Terri prove, sometimes it just makes more sense to rent than to buy. It all depends on your specific circumstances, where you live, and how long you're planning to stay there. Above all, you should always take all the options into account before buying a home. Keep your eyes fixed on the horizon—the breakeven horizon, that is—and, as always, let the data be your guide.

Exterior of a Hobbit Hole in the Shire *(Xinua/Photoshot)*

3

2-4-6-8, Neighborhoods That Will Appreciate

Predicting the Next Hot Spot

If we've learned one thing from the movies, it's that there are no clear-cut rules when it comes to time travel. Sometimes you need a flux capacitor to journey decades into the past. Other times you only need a tricked-out phone booth. Nevertheless, in almost every film where a character goes back in time, there is one common scene. At some point in history, the hero doles out some advice. "Buy Apple stock," they say to the people of the past—or, sometimes, to their own younger selves. "Oh, and you should definitely save your baseball cards."

But what if you could go back in time and use your knowledge of what's going to happen in the real estate market? You could tell your younger self to buy a house in that cheap, run-down part of town—because you know that it's going to be a chic, expensive neighborhood in just twenty years.

We haven't perfected time travel just yet, but we might have discovered the next best thing. By analyzing our data, we can pinpoint patterns that tell us whether—and how quickly—a neighborhood's homes are likely to increase in value in the future. The factors that determine these patterns range from the basic (proximity to downtown) to the controversial (gentrification) to the surprising (the age of a neighborhood's housing stock). Keep them in mind and you won't need the older, wiser version of yourself to appear in a flying blue box with real estate secrets. With these insights, you can be wiser today—and buy the best possible home for tomorrow.

FUTURE LOCATION, FUTURE LOCATION, FUTURE LOCATION

When you're shopping for a new home, the conventional wisdom says you should pay attention to "location, location, location." But our data shows that this familiar maxim is only half right. It's much more important to focus on "future location, future location, future location."

We don't have to convince you that buying a home is a huge commitment—financially, emotionally, and yes, geographically, too. It's a commitment that lasts years or decades into the future. That's true whether you plan to live in your new house indefinitely, or whether you plan to use it as an investment. And so the changes that will take place around a home will ultimately define its value much more than whatever the neighborhood looks like on the day you sign the mortgage papers.

In other words, the best real estate strategy isn't necessarily to buy a home in the most desirable part of town. Sometimes, the best strategy is to buy a home in the neighborhood that's going to *become* the most desirable part of town. That might sound like impossible advice to follow without a time machine. But looking deeply at our data, we can actually make very strong predictions about which neighborhoods are most likely to see increasing home values over time.

There are complex factors that cause these colossal shifts in neighborhoods and home values. But our analysis made one fact clear: These transformations are not at all random. Real estate values in and around major cities follow clear patterns as they change over a period of years or decades. More to the point, they follow patterns that we can *predict*—and that buyers can and should take into account before buying a home.

DOES CLOSER TO DOWNTOWN MEAN
FASTER APPRECIATION?

In most metro regions, homes near a city's center are the most valuable—and they often stay that way. They have an advantage over other neighborhoods because they offer shorter commute times, and because they tend to be overflowing with the great restaurants, art galleries, parks, cafés, and other neighborhood perks for which home buyers are willing to pay a premium. Even if the houses in the city center aren't any nicer than those at the outskirts, they will almost always sell for considerably more, just because their surrounding neighborhood adds value. If you meander out even a few blocks or miles, home values begin dropping, and they continue to fall steadily as you move away from the city center.

Our data shows that the homes in areas adjacent to the city center often tend to gain value much more quickly than homes in the city center. In other words, the gap between homes in central neighborhoods and outlying neighborhoods tends to shrink as the years go on.

The following graph of home price data in Phoenix illustrates the way that outlying homes become much more valuable compared to where they started. Each bar in this chart represents a distance of 10 miles from the city center. As you can see, a home 30 to 40 miles from the center of Phoenix went from being worth one-tenth to over forty percent of the value of a home in the city center over the course of thirty years.

The same phenomenon holds true in Dallas from 1970 to 2000. Homes 20 to 30 miles from the city center went from being worth 39 percent to just over 60 percent of the value of homes near the city center by the year 2000. We also see a similar phenomenon in Chicago from 1970 to 1990 and in Philadelphia from 1980 to 1990. However, it's important to note that the pattern isn't similar across time in all metro areas.

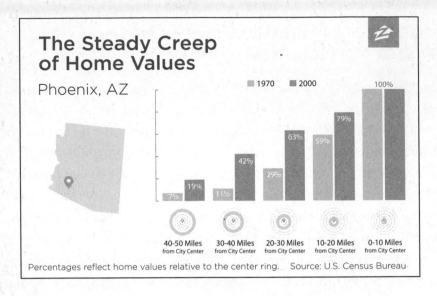

The Steady Creep of Home Values

Phoenix, AZ

■ 1970 ■ 2000

40-50 Miles from City Center	30-40 Miles from City Center	20-30 Miles from City Center	10-20 Miles from City Center	0-10 Miles from City Center
7% / 19%	11% / 42%	29% / 63%	59% / 79%	100% / 100%

Percentages reflect home values relative to the center ring. Source: U.S. Census Bureau

In Phoenix, if you could rewind back to 1970, it would be good advice to buy that house on the outskirts of town, as homes 20 to 30 miles outside of the city went from being worth roughly 30 percent of the value of homes near the city center to being worth 63 percent. So before you buy a condo right in the middle of the city, remember that home values will usually radiate out from the city center over time.

Still, these concentric circles don't fully explain why many formerly sub-par neighborhoods grow into home-value powerhouses. That process just happens to be occurring *within* the rings—and is complicated by many factors that go beyond simple distance from the city center.

WAIT FOR THE COOL TO COME TO YOU

As we delved further into the data, we found that a home's value is only partly a function of how far removed it is from the city center. In fact, *within* the concentric rings that surround a city's downtown, we found hot spots that appreciate *even more quickly* than the surrounding areas. If you can identify these hot spots, then you can have a fairly clear idea of precisely where housing values are going to be supercharged in the future.

The easiest way to find a hot spot is to look at one of the neighborhoods that has already taken off. As we pointed out earlier, people are willing to pay a premium to live in the kind of neighborhood that has restaurants, cafés, parks, and an enviable nightlife. But plenty of people also are willing to live in the next neighborhood over, where they still can access these advantages while enjoying cheaper housing.

As more and more people set down roots in those surrounding neighborhoods, enterprising chefs and coffee enthusiasts will start opening businesses to cater to this new clientele. There will almost inevitably be a cultural spillover from the premier neighborhood into the adjacent one. Ultimately, the entire area around a premier neighborhood will develop much more quickly than it otherwise would have. At Zillow, we call this the "halo effect."

Because these surrounding neighborhoods tend to be somewhat underdeveloped, their home values have quite a bit of room to grow. As a result, once they take off, their constituent homes tend to appreciate in value even more quickly than the homes in the premier neighborhood. Once again, it's actually a better real estate strategy to buy homes *outside* of the premier neighborhood.

So, if you're a savvy home buyer, you might want to move into one of the less developed neighborhoods surrounding that awesome part of town. You can pretty safely bet that, in time, you'll enjoy both a higher home value and a neighborhood with many of the same features that you once had to travel for. In short, if you have a little patience, you can wait for the cool to come to you.

This isn't true in every city—but the evidence shows a strong halo effect in cities as diverse as New York, Charlotte, and Chicago.

Take New York as an example. In 1997, the premier neighborhood in New York City was Tribeca. There, home values were an average of almost three times that of the city taken as a whole. Right next door to Tribeca was SoHo, which was also filled with homes much more valuable than the rest of the city—over two and a half times the city median home value.

Right nearby, however, several neighborhoods had much lower home values than the rest of the city. Just across the East River, median home values in Brooklyn's DUMBO neighborhood were only 72 percent of the city median. Yet, during the next fifteen years, the appreciation in this once "sub-par" neighborhood far outpaced the premier neighborhoods. Home values in DUMBO grew 617 percent over the fifteen years from 1997 to 2012, 65 percent faster than Tribeca, which only grew 374 percent over the same period.

We see the same pattern in Chicago and in Charlotte. The neighborhoods surrounding the premier areas may have been less valuable, but their value grew much, much more quickly.

It's worth noting that we did not find a halo effect in every city. In Seattle, for instance, neighborhoods surrounding the premier neighborhood of Laurelhurst did not necessarily grow any faster. This is most likely because Seattle is a much more homogenous city than others we analyzed. The areas surrounding Laurelhurst were already fairly affluent—so there was less opportunity for people who wanted cheap access to the premier neighborhood to go house-hunting there.

Of course, you don't necessarily have to be physically close to a premier neighborhood to see appreciation. The premier neighborhood must be easily accessible for the halo effect to take effect. That's why so many of the New York neighborhoods that showed such outsized growth were located along subway and rail lines. They might have been separated from Tribeca by the East River, but as the map on the next page demonstrates, the easy access to mass transit was enough to get them the spillover from the best neighborhoods in town.

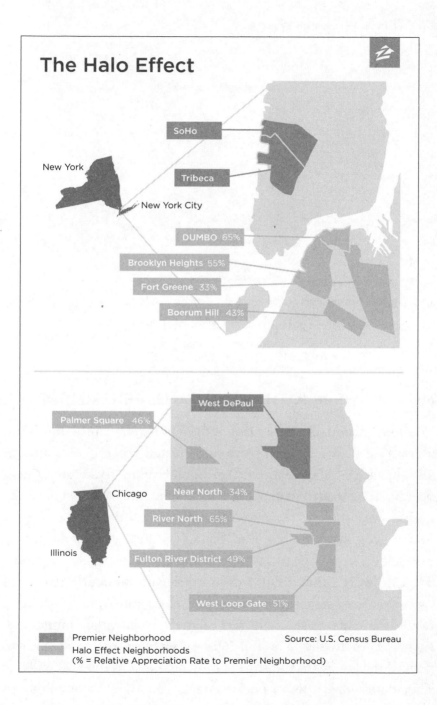

The Halo Effect

New York

New York City

SoHo

Tribeca

DUMBO 65%

Brooklyn Heights 55%

Fort Greene 33%

Boerum Hill 43%

West DePaul

Palmer Square 46%

Chicago

Near North 34%

River North 65%

Illinois

Fulton River District 49%

West Loop Gate 51%

Premier Neighborhood

Halo Effect Neighborhoods
(% = Relative Appreciation Rate to Premier Neighborhood)

Source: U.S. Census Bureau

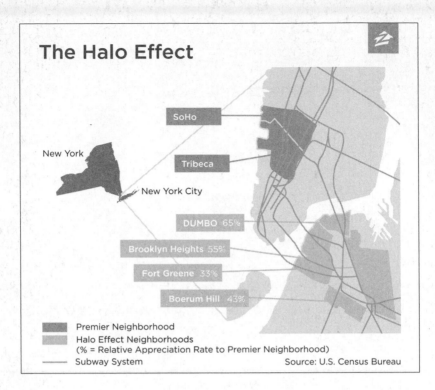

MORE POWERFUL THAN THE HALO: GENTRIFICATION

The Halo Effect changes neighborhoods through proximity and access. But there's an even more complicated process that can rapidly change neighborhoods and send home values rocketing: gentrification. It's a loaded, complicated term, and it represents one of the most powerful forces shaping American cities today.

To get a sense of how this process unfolds, let's consider an example from the past: the East Village, a now trendy neighborhood in lower Manhattan. In the nineteenth and early twentieth centuries, the neighborhood was a bustling immigrant port. As a result, the rents were low in this relatively residential community. Fast-forward to the '50s and '60s, when beatniks from uptown noticed the low rents and started moving down to the East Village. They didn't have a lot of pocket change, and they were willing to trade some inconvenience for their own bedrooms in a reasonably sized apartment—even if it hadn't been renovated in years. The neighborhood might have been out of the way, but the low rents were just too good to pass up.

Then, in the '60s and '70s, this first wave of urban pioneers began calling their friends—the hippies, the musicians, the artists. "You have to move out here!" they said. "We split the rent three ways and it's practically free. We even have room for a home studio!" More and more young people came for the low rents, and they stayed for the community that they built together. Before long, bars, restaurants, art galleries, clubs, and many more staples started to appear in the neighborhood to cater to this new community. The iconic punk rock venue CBGB, for instance, opened in the East Village in 1973. The first wavers were thrilled. They started bragging to their friends about how cool, and how cheap, their neighborhood was. More of their friends—and friends of friends—started to show up.

By the '90s, the neighborhood was still evolving, shedding some of its counterculture mystique, and making way for yet another wave of new residents. Local real estate firms and investors began to see an opportunity. They knew a lot of people would pay a premium to live in such a hotbed of culture—but only if the housing stock became significantly nicer. So developers seized the moment and started buying up buildings. They renovated them—totally gutted them in some cases—and set the stage for yet another wave of change.

With the neighborhood transforming rapidly, even the homes that hadn't been extensively renovated had skyrocketing home values. Rents shot up right along with them. These homes became sufficiently expensive that most of the original tenants—along with the previous waves of gentrifiers—were eventually pushed out. They moved elsewhere in search of new, inexpensive housing. Before long, a whole new group of people was living in the East Village.

This process paved the way for the neighborhood to become fully gentrified. Upper-middle class residents—the "gentry"—are now drawn to live in the area. Of course, these people never would have considered living in that very neighborhood during the early stages of gentrification. But now, this formerly low-income neighborhood is home to young professionals, well-to-do families, and wealthy artists and designers. Home values have jumped sky-high as a result.

Of course, the ramifications of gentrification go far beyond real estate. There are questions of race, class, money, and politics that are inextricably linked to the conversation about gentrification. Today, the benefits and drawbacks of gentrification are being hotly debated in neighborhoods all across the country, most notably in San Francisco's historic Mission District.

Skeptics are quick to point out that while the forces of gentrification may carry a massive influx of wealth, new money doesn't usually benefit the people who have lived there for years. In the face of swelling rent and property taxes, locals—almost always low-income and usually members of minority groups—are forced to confront the difficult decision of paying more to stay or uprooting their lives. Critics also lament the installation of chain stores in place of long-standing small businesses. "How many neighborhood coffee shops have been replaced with a Starbucks?" they ask.

Still, plenty of people are happy when the Starbucks moves in—and not only developers and landlords (and for good reason, as we'll explore in the next chapter). For residents who own their homes in these neighborhoods, gentrification brings a windfall of wealth. Residents who are able to stay also benefit from new investments in infrastructure, roads, schools, and parks. Neighborhoods tend to become safer, and new business developments in these neighborhoods bring new job opportunities along with them. Adam Sternbergh summed up this viewpoint in a *New York* magazine article headlined "What's Wrong With Gentrification?," arguing, "Often lost amid our caricatures of benighted hipsters invading a blighted neighborhood is the fact that without gentrification, you've simply got a blighted neighborhood."

These are complicated questions with strong voices and valid arguments on each side. We don't claim to provide any easy answers. But using our data, we *do* have some new insights into the forces that drive gentrification.

FORGET ABOUT HIPSTERS, LOOK AT HOUSING STOCK

Above all, our data made one thing clear: The process of gentrification is not random. The seeds of rapid redevelopment, in many neighborhoods, are often planted twenty or thirty years before the effects become clear.

In general, neighborhoods are most likely to gentrify if they have older homes, low homeownership rates, and some access to more popular neighborhoods. Factors like the local population's median income and education level are correlated as well, but, believe it or not, they are much weaker indicators for eventual gentrification.

To find the harbingers of gentrification, we first identified the sub-par neighborhoods that appreciated the most from December 2002 to December 2012 in cities across the country. (We considered "sub-par" to mean any neighborhood in which the median home value was at least 10 percent less than the city's overall median home value.)

Once we identified these neighborhoods, we examined their histories to see what they had in common.

Above all, the greatest indicator for a neighborhood that would one day strongly appreciate in value was the age of its housing stock. The older the average home is, the more likely a given neighborhood will see strong appreciation. When a sub-par neighborhood had more than 17 percent of its homes over 40 years old in 1980, then it would appreciate faster than half the neighborhoods in the county 47 percent of the time. On the flip side, a neighborhood with mostly new housing (less than 17 percent over the age of 40) only had a 24 percent chance of appreciating faster than the rest of the county.

This makes sense, because if the average home is much older, that also means it has the most room for improvement. In general, the age of housing stock helps us see the gap between what the neighborhood is and what it could be if it were fixed up. So if you're looking for a home that's likely to have outsized appreciation in the future, you'll do well to buy a home in a sub-par neighborhood of older homes.

However, measuring appreciation alone doesn't give a full picture of gentrification. After all, gentrification is a process of reinvestment and change writ large. It's not just about rising home values. So we developed an index that takes into account not only appreciation, but also variables like changes in medium income and the rate of new investment, offering a richer picture of gentrification

In New York City, it's no surprise that our formula spotlights several sure-bet neighborhoods like Carroll Gardens and Park Slope. But it also points to some hidden gems, like Sunset Park, a historically Hispanic section of southern Brooklyn that features beautiful, old brownstones and sweeping views of New York Harbor; or Clason Point, a waterfront section of the Bronx with single-family homes, many covered in distinctive aluminum siding.

Applying the same index to Los Angeles and Chicago returned similar results, identifying some trendy and rapidly gentrifying neighborhoods, like Echo Park, just north of downtown LA, and the South Commons in Chicago.

Once again, we went back in time to analyze what characteristics these neighborhoods had in common. This time, the strongest common indicator was a low rate of homeownership by the people who actually live in the neighborhood. Neighborhoods with low homeowner-occupation in 1980 were much more likely to gentrify in the future. In part, this was because the people who *did* own these properties were much more open to selling to developers. That way, developers had an easier time moving in and renovating the housing stock.

As you can see, the factors that predict gentrification are complex, and our data showed that they vary by state. But it's important to remember that, more than anything else, they are measures of potential. Neighborhoods in many city centers have been growing for years, and can probably only make marginal improvements. But neighborhoods with very old homes—and therefore plenty of homes with renovation potential—have a lot of room to grow. Therefore, if you're looking for a neighborhood where home values will appreciate rapidly someday, look for old housing stock and low homeownership rates.

LEARNING FROM HISTORY, PREDICTING THE FUTURE

Remember that sign on your high school history class wall: "Those who cannot remember the past are condemned to repeat it." It turns out that this adage is only partly true. We *can* learn from the past, but we might repeat it anyway. With history's lessons in hand, the future becomes a much more predictable place.

If you're looking for a home in the next big neighborhood, it really is possible to find it ten, twenty, or even thirty years in advance—and without a time machine. You just need to look for old housing stock. Look for a place that's not too far from the action. Look for a neighborhood with a low rate of homeownership.

If you buy a home in that neighborhood, the odds are that you'll see some major home appreciation coming your way. You just have to sit back and let the future come to you.

Interior of the set of Frasier Crane's living room from the TV show *Frasier* (*Joey Delvalle/NBC/NBCU Photo Bank via Getty Images*)

The Starbucks Effect

How Lattes Perk Up Home Prices

Now that you know about gentrification, you may be wondering what fuels it. The answer is, the same thing that fuels the rest of us: coffee.

But not just any old cup o' joe.

Starbucks, the iconic coffee roaster and retailer, has grown into a $15 billion company, with more than 19,000 locations in more than sixty countries.[1] You can spot that familiar green-and-white logo from Saudi Arabia to Switzerland, in a Dubai shopping mall, or on a Carnival Cruise ship. Where the Berlin Wall once stood, there's a shiny new Starbucks instead.[2] Conveniently, Spencer's desk has a view of the original Starbucks store in Pike Place Market.

Starbucks' mission is "to inspire and nurture the human spirit—one person, one cup and one neighborhood at a time."[3] Any college student downing Venti Caramel Macchiatos to stay awake the night before a big exam can testify to Starbucks', in a word, *nurturing* qualities. But as it turns out, Starbucks correlates with something else, too: rising home values.

To explore exactly how closely the two correlate, we compared a database of Starbucks locations with Zillow data. And since Starbucks' corporate headquarters in Seattle is located just a few miles down the road from Zillow, we also took the opportunity to pay our neighbors a visit, and to pick the brains of Starbucks' own real estate analytics team—the whizzes who determine where to put that next Starbucks location.

Here's what we can tell you: Starbucks equates with Venti-sized home-value appreciation. Moreover, Starbucks seems to be fueling—not following—these higher home values.

And the reason why is that Starbucks' real estate choices are, in their words, "as much an art as a science." When deciding where to hang their next shingle, they marry right-brain ingenuity with hard-headed, left-brain analysis—exactly as you should.

Let's take these fresh-brewed insights one at a time.

STARBUCKS EQUALS BIG BUCKS

Although some may scoff that the predictive value of a given retail chain doesn't mean much, locations near Starbucks are, indisputably, highly lucrative.

True, properties near Starbucks locations tend to start out more expensive. But as you can see, these properties appreciate at a faster rate than US housing on the whole. Interestingly, they're also recovering much more quickly from the housing bust.

What does that look like in practice? Let's look at the historical home value appreciation of areas that now are located within a quarter mile of a Starbucks. A home that is now near a Starbucks would have sold, on average, for $137,000. A home that is not near a Starbucks would have sold, on average, for $102,000.

Fast-forward seventeen years to 2014. That average American home has now appreciated 65 percent, to $168,000. But the Starbucks-adjacent property has far outpaced that, appreciating 96 percent to $269,000.

STARBUCKS IS THE FUEL, NOT THE FOLLOWER

"Try some decaf," you may be thinking. "Home prices rise and fall for a lot of reasons. How do we know this has anything to do with

Starbucks?" For instance, maybe this isn't a Starbucks Effect at all. Maybe it's just a coffee shop effect.

To examine that possibility, we took a look at another prominent coffee chain, Dunkin' Donuts.

What did we learn? Homes near Dunkin' Donuts reflect a similar historical trend. But while they appreciate faster than the nation's housing as a whole, they still don't appreciate as fast as properties that are now a quarter mile from a Starbucks.

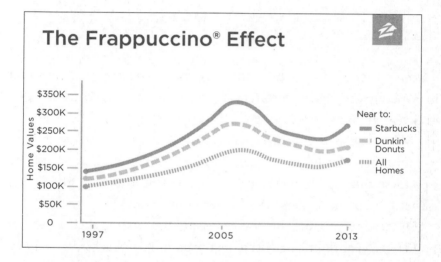

In fact, between 1997 and 2012, homes now located near Starbucks and Dunkin' Donuts followed similar historical trajectories, substantially outpacing the overall home value appreciation. But their paths diverged during the recent housing recovery such that, today, homes near Dunkin' Donuts have appreciated 80 percent since 1997 whereas homes near Starbucks have appreciated 96 percent, almost doubling their value.

Even so, you may be saying, is it possible that the Starbucks Effect is really just a Coastal Effect? Or an Urban Effect?

Maybe people really like living in Seattle and Boston, and the Starbucks locations dotting their neighborhoods are just incidental. We wondered this, too. After all, when we looked at a map of

Home Values: Starbucks vs. Dunkin' Donuts

Home Types	1997 to Peak (April 2007)	Peak to Bottom (April 2007 to Jan 2012)	1997 to 2013
All Properties	92%	49%	65%
Near a Starbucks	139%	67%	96%
Near a Dunkin' Donuts	136%	70%	80%

Starbucks locations in the United States, it's readily apparent that historically they have clustered on the coasts, in the Midwest, and in urban areas.

Moreover, maybe Starbucks and Dunkin' Donuts are just waiting for a neighborhood's property values to heat up before moving in and setting up shop. What's to say that Starbucks is the cause, rather than a consequence, of higher home values?

To attempt to rule out these possibilities, we tracked values of homes in a very tight ring within a quarter mile of Starbucks (so close you could practically smell the dark roast from your front porch) and compared those very-Starbucks-adjacent homes to houses slightly farther away, in a ring of homes between a quarter- and a half-mile from a Starbucks. And we compared home values in these two rings (adjacent and nearby) for only the five years after the Starbucks location actually opened, in order to see whether the effect took place after the opening or already existed before the store opened.

Lo and behold, the adjacent homes beat out the nearby homes. Those houses closest to Starbucks appreciated a little more than 21 percent over 5 years, while the houses slightly farther away only appreciated just less than 17 percent. So, yes, some of the difference is related to the location itself, but there's still a healthy difference attributable to the arrival of a Starbucks.

Whatever the reasons—because they genuinely like drinking coffee, or because they see Starbucks as a proxy for gentrification—it seems pretty clear that people are paying a premium for homes near Starbucks. And furthermore, it looks like Starbucks itself is driving the increase in home values.

PICKING LOCATIONS: AN ART AND A SCIENCE

Armed with this data, we headed down Seattle's First Avenue to Starbucks HQ. There, we had the pleasure of chatting with Arthur Rubinfeld, who oversees Starbucks' location-selection process, and his extremely talented team. We asked them, is the Starbucks Effect the product of careful, data-driven decisions on their part? And their answer was, more or less, yes.

The Starbucks team explained that while they have twenty or so analytics experts around the world poring over maps and geographic information systems data—assessing factors like an area's traffic patterns and businesses—the company also empowers dozens of regional teams to come to their own conclusions about location, store design, and a host of other issues.

Yet, even with their reams of data and locally driven decision-making, our Starbucks friends noted that there was no single silver bullet. "The beauty of Starbucks is our understanding of real-estate site locationing," Arthur told us. "It's an art and a science."

We couldn't have put it better ourselves.

There have been times and places—like before the financial crisis, when Starbucks bet on an up-and-coming Seattle commercial area that never materialized—where the art of site location is displayed in all of its messiness. In other instances, the science has delivered big-time returns.

Ultimately, one Starbucks pro told us, "We try to provide consistency in the science...so that local decision makers have everything they need at their fingertips to make easy decisions."

That, in a nutshell, is exactly the purpose of this book. We do the science so that you are armed with the best possible information to make smart and easy decisions. Because at the end of the day, where you buy a home is based on countless subjective factors. As in *Moby-Dick*—whose pages gave us the first mate Starbuck and inspired the Starbucks name—finding that perfect, ahead-of-the-curve home can sometimes seem like chasing your very own white whale. But we're here with the numbers to make that search a little bit easier. So, grab a Venti Skim Latte—hey, get the extra shot—and go find the right home for you.

Exterior of home from the movie *Amityville Horror* (Courtesy Everett Collection)

5

It's the Worst House for a Reason

Why You Shouldn't *Buy the Worst House in the Best Neighborhood*

Some proverbs offer sage counsel. A bird in the hand is worth two in the bush. Cleanliness is next to godliness. Even a broken watch is right twice a day. Luck is what happens when preparation meets opportunity. These are wise words to live by. But one saying that needs to have its proverbial status revoked is the well-known real estate adage, "Buy the worst house in the best neighborhood."

Proponents of this strategy contend that buying a bad house in a good neighborhood is a surefire investment. The higher value of the surrounding homes, the argument goes, will elevate even the worst home's value. A great neighborhood is like a rising tide: It will lift the price of *all* the houses in it.

This advice has been offered, exaggerated, and accepted for decades.

As far back as the late 1970s, newspapers have profiled investors who cite their worst-house-in-the-best-neighborhood strategy as the guiding principle of the real estate game.[1]

In 1987, a *Chicago Tribune* article, entitled "Buy the Worst House on the Street," asked readers, "Would you spend $1 to make $2?"

In 2010, Rich M. bought a fixer-upper in Seattle's Capitol Hill neighborhood. After renovating it, he sent the before and after pictures to the home improvement magazine *This Old House*, winning a spot as a finalist in the annual Reader Remodel Contest. The pictures ran with the caption—what else?—"Worst House in Best Neighborhood."[2]

Even British artist David Hockney shared his opinion on the matter: "Always live in the ugliest house on the street—then you don't have to look at it."[3]

From CNN Money, to Investopedia, to the late Robert Bruss (known as the "Dear Abby" of real estate), the so-called experts have done their best to convince the rest of us that purchasing the best possible neighborhood's worst house is a smart move.

But are they right? Is buying the worst house in the best neighborhood a wise investment or is this strategy a real estate myth?

Here's how we used data to separate truth from adage.

Step one was to take a hard look at the cheapest 10 percent of homes in a given ZIP code. We wanted to start with a real understanding of what buyers are getting when they purchase a home that is priced well below a neighborhood's median value. So we compared the appreciation rates of the bottom 10 percent against the rest of the homes in their respective ZIP codes. This let us see how the bottom 10 percent of homes performs relative to those of their neighbors.

If the adage were true, the bottom 10 percent of houses would need to perform *better* than the more expensive homes in their neighborhood. Faster appreciation would indicate that buying the cheapest house in the best neighborhood is a strategy that really does pays off.

But—alas—it doesn't.

Instead, we found that only rarely does the bottom 10 percent outperform the top 90 percent of houses in a ZIP code. On average, these bottom-tier homes do neither better nor worse than the others.

Looking at those numbers, we might have concluded that

buying a neighborhood's worst home is therefore a neutral invest-ment strategy—a myth, but not a harmful one. It doesn't *maximize* returns. But it doesn't *cost* buyers either.

Then, however, we dug a little deeper—and we saw that buying the worst house in the best neighborhood can actually backfire. That's because the more affluent a neighborhood is, relative to its greater metropolitan area, the worse the homes in its bottom 10 percent tend to perform.

In short, the nicer the neighborhood, the bigger the myth!

Take the case of two imaginary families in the Dallas metro area twenty years ago: the Neimans and the Marcuses. Both were scouring the market for a new home.

The Neimans were young, in love, and hadn't amassed much in the way of savings. In fact, they weren't even sure they could afford to buy. But then they found it: the perfect little bungalow in Eagle Ranch, a suburban neighborhood in Fort Worth. Sure, the house was in the bottom 10 percent of houses in the neighborhood. But the neighboring houses were so great!

Meanwhile, the Marcuses had been saving a little longer and were in a position to make a larger investment in a more expensive house. They could easily afford one of the nicer properties in Eagle Ranch, but instead, they decided to buy one of the worst homes in North Dallas, a more affluent neighborhood than Eagle Ranch. It wasn't their dream home. But they figured that the pricier surround-ing homes would pull the property value up. After all, Mr. Marcus told Mrs. Marcus, "You should always buy the worst house in the best neighborhood!"

You probably can guess what happened to the Neimans in Eagle Ranch. Even as the rest of the homes in their neighborhood appreci-ated in value, their house continued to lag behind by about 4 percent-age points.

But that's not nearly as bad as what happened in North Dallas. There, the Marcuses watched in horror as their home under-performed its neighbors *by a whopping 20 percentage points.*[4]

In other words, neither family found buying the worst house in the best neighborhood to be a winning investment strategy. But it turned out even worse for the Marcuses in North Dallas.

All of which raises an interesting question: Why does the bottom 10 percent of homes perform worse in a better neighborhood? The likeliest explanation is that there is less demand for lower-priced homes in nicer neighborhoods. As one might expect, in fancy areas, fancy homes are in the highest demand.

Imagine, for example, that you're trying to sell a $375,000 co-op in Park Slope, a neighborhood on the western side of Brooklyn, which the *New York Times* described a few years ago as "both haunt and hatchery of New York's smuggest limousine-liberal yuppies."[5] The median list price of a Park Slope home is typically six times the national average—and *twice* the price of the co-op in question. And buyers there aren't messing around.

When you bought this house, you were so excited about finding a Park Slope home you could afford that you were willing to look past the fact that it was a dump. And, with the help of a contractor, you've made it much more livable. So you can't understand why buyers aren't biting. "Can't they see what a steal this is?" you ask.

Unfortunately for you, the truth is that buyers in Park Slope aren't looking for a $375,000 co-op. They're in another stratosphere. A $375,000 co-op isn't even on their radar. And even if they somehow stumbled upon a home that cheap, they *might* be excited. More likely, however, they'd wonder what the heck was wrong with it.

And therein lies the rub. Because the people who follow this advice do so right in the very neighborhoods where the bottom 10 percent of homes will deliver the worst relative performance. By buying the worst house in the best neighborhood, they're also buying the worst house where it has the *worst chance* of appreciating in value.

BUY THE WORST HOUSE IN THE HOTTEST NEIGHBORHOOD

It's become clichéd in itself to say that clichés endure because they represent truths. But given how deeply this myth has penetrated real estate investors' philosophy, we figured there must be *something* substantiated about it. So we asked: Is there anywhere that a buyer *can* purchase a home in the bottom 10 percent and still turn a profit?

The answer is yes, there *are* conditions under which the bottom 10 percent of houses can outperform the neighborhood as a whole. But these aren't the worst houses in the best neighborhoods; they're the worst houses in the *hottest* neighborhoods. In a hot neighborhood, even the bottom 10 percent of homes can turn a cool profit.

So what's a hot neighborhood? It's an up-and-coming area that has seen five consecutive years of higher-than-average home value appreciation. If you get to one of these neighborhoods within the first five years of it becoming hot, you have a chance of snatching a property at a low price point that, with some tender loving care, will soon reach the mean of the ZIP code. This especially is true in gentrifying neighborhoods where demand for higher density development such as condos and apartments drives up prices for cheaper properties.

Now Pittsburgh, Pennsylvania, may not be the first place you think of when you hear about a hot trend. But, using data from 2008 on, we can see that Pittsburgh's historic district of Manchester is seeing this exact phenomenon play out.

At the turn of the twentieth century, Manchester was a prosperous enclave of steel barons and other mansion dwellers. While some of their historic homes remain intact, many of them fell into disrepair as Manchester residents fled for the suburbs. But, by many accounts, the neighborhood is on the rise, experiencing a renaissance that is ushering in its second golden era.[6] And, during the past five years, Manchester property values have been skyrocketing.

Let's imagine another hypothetical family, the Roethlisbergers, die-hard Steelers fans, who are looking for a fixer-upper to transform into their dream house. They've heard stories about triumphant homeowners who have scooped up older Manchester properties on the cheap and restored them to their former glory. And so they buy one of the homes they can afford—which, of course, is valued in the bottom 10 percent of Manchester's homes.

Unlike the Neimans and Marcuses, the Roethlisbergers' story has a happy ending. Manchester is so hot that the bottom 10 percent of homes are not only keeping pace with the rest of the neighborhood; they're outperforming the more expensive homes by an average of 4 percentage points. On the banks of the Ohio River, a Cinderella story has come true: The worst house in the best neighborhood has turned a profit.

Unfortunately, even in hot neighborhoods like Manchester, investing in one of those bottom 10 percent homes only works if your timing is absolutely perfect. Missing the boat can be extremely costly, because in neighborhoods where appreciation has slowed after an initial spike, the bottom 10 percent of homes tend to underperform compared to the neighborhood average.

In other words, if you don't get to the neighborhood while it's still hot, any cheap house you buy will likely do even worse than homes in the bottom 10 percent generally do.

We have a couple of theories about that, as well. One explanation is that a period of initial appreciation in a neighborhood can simply be a "false start"—an expected boom that quickly becomes a bust. People *thought* the neighborhood was going to be hot, but, for whatever reason, they were wrong.

Another explanation is that, after a fast start, the market is picked over. By then, all of the neighborhood's investment or redevelopment opportunities have been exhausted—and the properties that are still cheap are cheap for a reason. Any home that could be replaced with high-density housing has already been identified, sold, and bulldozed to make way for a new building. This means the homes that are left are either in a horrible location or in such bad condition that no small amount of work will elevate their value to the mean of the ZIP code.

In short, they're not going to provide a great return on investment.

The Las Vegas Strip is an example of one of the worst neighborhoods in which to own the worst home. While the Strip once *was* a hot neighborhood, due to its proximity to many casinos and tourist attractions, its luck eventually went cold, as luck in Vegas is wont to do. Now, the bottom 10 percent of homes in the area are underperforming the rest of the neighborhood by a solid 9 percentage points. And buyers who took a gamble on one of those worst homes have learned the hard way that even in Vegas, the house doesn't always win.

Which brings us back to those kindly folks who always seem to have an aphorism for every occasion.

Sometimes they're not wrong. But that doesn't always mean they're right.

Here's what the data says: Buy a decent house in the *right* neighborhood. What's the right neighborhood? It's the most expensive one where you can afford a home that is *not* in the bottom 10 percent.

The Cosby family in their living room from the TV show *The Cosby Show* (NBC/ *Photofest*)

Do Your Homework

Finding a Great School District
in Your Price Range

When buyers are shopping for a new home, they're oftentimes shopping for a new school district, too. In fact, in one survey, 91 percent of respondents said that school boundaries were an important part of finding the perfect home.[1]

As the proud parents of school-aged kids, we couldn't agree more.

Generally speaking, high-quality schools go hand-in-hand with high property values, and it's easy to see why. Once folks learn about the quality of the local schools, demand for homes in that school district will drive up property values.

At the same time, since most US schools are funded by state and local property taxes, living in an expensive area—holding everything else constant—means that higher property taxes generate more revenue for local schools. The result is that expenditures per student can vary widely among schools in the same area, with schools in more expensive neighborhoods receiving more money to spend on hiring teachers, building nice facilities, and buying new computers for the classroom.

In other words, great school districts boost property values, and high property values boost school quality. That's why most people try to buy a house in the best school district they can afford.

But how do you figure that out? It's hard to do on your own, which is why Zillow created a unique dataset that matches school quality data to local home values. The school ratings data comes from GreatSchools, a national leader in providing school performance data to parents. GreatSchools compares the most recent available state standardized test results of schools, and then ranks the schools from 1 (the lowest) to 10 (the highest).[2]

We found that the states with the weakest relationship between home values and school quality—meaning they offer more egalitarian public education—are South Carolina, New York, and New Mexico. In other words, if you're a New Mexico homeowner whose house is in the bottom 10 percent of home values statewide, the caliber of your kid's school is fairly close to the quality of the schools in New Mexico's most expensive neighborhoods.

By contrast, the Rust Belt states of Ohio, Pennsylvania, and Michigan exhibit the strongest correlation between school quality and home values. In Michigan, for example, homeowners in the bottom 10 percent can expect schools ranking a relatively dismal 2.1 on the GreatSchools scale. At the same time, wealthier Michigan neighborhoods—places like Bloomfield Hills, an affluent suburb of Detroit—can boast schools rating a sky-high 9.2 on the GreatSchools ranking.

At higher home values and school ratings, the strength of the relationship actually increases. In Pennsylvania, for example, moving from a GreatSchools rating of 5 to 6 requires a 15.4 percent increase in home values. But moving from an 8 to a 9 requires a 60.1 percent increase in home values. In other words, to go from an average school district to a slightly better one doesn't cost very much—but to go from a great school district to an excellent one costs an awful lot. That's also the case in California, where jumping from a 5- to a 6-rated school district only requires a 9.9 percent increase in home value, compared to a 47.9 percent increase to move from an 8 to a 9 on the GreatSchools scale.

The practical implications of this are clear and welcome: On

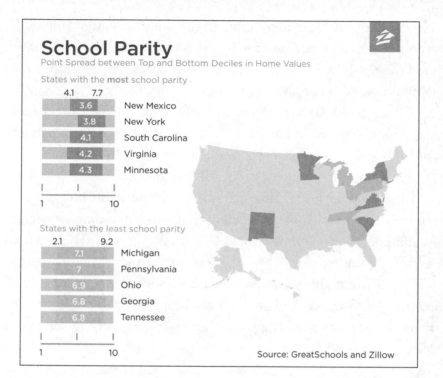

School Parity
Point Spread between Top and Bottom Deciles in Home Values

States with the **most** school parity

3.6	New Mexico
3.8	New York
4.1	South Carolina
4.2	Virginia
4.3	Minnesota

4.1   7.7

1   10

States with the least school parity

7.1	Michigan
7	Pennsylvania
6.9	Ohio
6.8	Georgia
6.8	Tennessee

2.1   9.2

1   10

Source: GreatSchools and Zillow

the lower end of the school quality spectrum, it's easier to "trade up" for marginally better schools without breaking the bank. But what about the elusive holy grail of real estate for buyers with kids: Is it possible to find high-quality public education in a much more affordable neighborhood?

To answer that question, we combined GreatSchools rankings with school district boundary information for elementary schools and high schools. Looking at the combined data, sure enough, we found that pricey neighborhoods aren't the only places with good schools. In fact, all across the country, you can find excellent schools in relatively cheap adjacent neighborhoods.

Consider, for example, Dublin, Ohio, a suburb of Columbus (and a popular stop on the PGA tour). Both Scottish Corners Elementary School and Deer Run Elementary are in the Dublin City School District, are rated as "10" elementary schools by GreatSchools, and are 2.6 miles apart. Both feed into Jerome High School, also a 10.

But while the median home value in the Deer Run attendance zone is $413,100, the median in the Scottish Corners attendance zone is only $286,400! Clearly, Scottish Corners gives you way more education bang for your housing buck.

Greer, South Carolina, a suburb of Greenville, is another great case study. Woodland Elementary School and Buena Vista Elementary are both 10s, and both feed into the highly rated Riverside High School. The elementary schools are only 2.3 miles apart, but the difference in home prices is dramatic. To attend Buena Vista, the median home value is $290,000. In the attendance zone for Woodland, the median is only $149,900. Again, there is more than a $100,000 difference in home values for the same school quality.

There are many affordable neighborhoods that feed into excellent school districts. And now, for the first time, you can easily find them. All it takes is a little bit of parental homework to send your kids to an A+ school—without spending too many Gs.

Tree houses from the movie *Swiss Family Robinson (Buena Vista Distribution Company/Photofest)*

ARMs and Legs

Fixed-Rate Mortgages Aren't for Everyone

Pants, the late postmodernist writer David Foster Wallace once observed, make no sense—at least not on men. Whether it's khaki slacks or denim jeans, expecting men to wear trousers, Wallace believed, is arbitrary and unfair, "based solely on archaic custom." In his view, pants are "not only incommodious but illogical" for a number of reasons: They ride up, they're hot, they chafe, and they are—shall we say—restrictive.[1]

"And yet," Wallace noted, "the fact remains that in the broad cultural mainstream of millennial America, men do not wear skirts. If you, the reader, are a US male, and even if you share my personal objections to pants and dream as I do of a cool and genitally unsquishy American Tomorrow, the odds are still 99.9 percent that in 100 percent of public situations you wear pants/slacks/shorts/trunks."[2]

In other words, American men wearing pants is a convention we don't question, something so culturally engrained it goes unremarked-upon, no matter how many reasons there might be to choose an alternative.

The same goes with mortgages.

Few standards are more universally accepted than the belief that you should buy your home with a thirty-year, fixed-rate mortgage. It's just what you do. In the US post–housing bubble, more than 80 percent of mortgages are fixed-rate. Even in the pre-bubble housing boom, the share of fixed-rate mortgages was never below 50 percent.

But there's a whole other world of mortgages out there—adjustable-rate mortgages, or ARMs. They come in different shapes and sizes, and they can save you a lot of money over a fixed-rate mortgage in certain instances. In this chapter, we're going to take a look at which mortgage is the better bet for the average home buyer.

But first, let's explore the somewhat bizarre phenomenon of the enormously popular thirty-year, fixed-rate mortgage (we'll call it the FRM, for short).

Think about it for a moment: Is there anything at all that Americans do for *thirty years*? Almost half of Americans change their religions, and usually before age twenty-four.[3] We leave our jobs, on average, after 4.6 years.[4] Before divorce, the average marriage in the United States lasts eight years.[5] And yet, consumers routinely make the most important financial decisions of their lives based on the assumption that they'll live in the same house for thirty years.

All of which begs the question: Are thirty-year FRMs the men's trousers of American real estate? Is it an arbitrary norm? Is it even logical? Why are we so enamored of the thirty-year mortgage, and is it really right for everyone?

Looking around the world, it's interesting to note that the United States is just about the only country with a thirty-year or longer fixed-rate mortgage with no-prepayment penalties (Denmark being another example). As much as we take the FRM for granted in the United States, globally speaking, it's anything but ordinary. France, for instance, only offers up to a twenty- to twenty-five-year term on fixed-rate mortgages due to heavy rental market subsidization and mortgage regulation. (Incidentally, the French originally gave us the word for "mortgage"—the literal translation is "dead pledge" in Old French.)[6]

Here in the United States, the government's involvement in the US mortgage market is the main reason why the thirty-year-fixed remains our standard. Left to their own devices, banks typically don't like to make thirty-year bets on what will happen to mortgage rates. And a thirty-year FRM requires banks not only to project potential interest rates far into the future, but also to allow the borrower to refinance anytime rates fall below the initial rate that the borrower accepted when the loan was first taken out. This means that borrowers can have their cake and eat it, too. They can lock in a rate today, but can always switch if a more attractive rate comes along later. This is great for borrowers, but not so great for banks, since banks lose money if rates go up more than they expect, but they don't get the opportunity to make more money if rates go down (because borrowers can refinance).

To make this arrangement palatable to banks, it's been necessary for the government to provide some guarantee in order to create incentives for banks to make fixed-rate mortgages widely available. This has taken the form of two government-sponsored enterprises, Fannie Mae and Freddie Mac, and other mortgage programs sponsored by the Federal Housing Administration and Veterans Administration, among others. As a result, the United States ranks highest among advanced economies in government participation in mortgage markets, according to a 2011 International Monetary Fund report.[7] That's right: The United States, a paragon of free market capitalism, has the highest government involvement in mortgage finance of any country on Earth.

Interestingly, the thirty-year mortgage emerged as something of an historical accident. It's remained common partly because it has more affordable payments than a shorter-term loan. But, in large part, the thirty-year mortgage is still common today simply *because* it's so common. That may sound like circular logic, but it's really just logic reinforced by a basic fact: Americans simply don't think that hard about what kind of mortgage they're going to get. In almost all cases, they just go with the most common, most obvious choice.

In fact, a recent Zillow survey found that the average American spends only five hours researching their mortgage options. Nearly one-third of all Americans spend two hours or less. Those numbers are especially striking when you consider that the average American spends five hours researching their next vacation. They spend an average of four hours researching a computer purchase. And most striking, they spend twice as much time—ten hours—doing research before they buy a car!

It's amazing to think that many Americans spend weeks and months searching for the perfect home, but then devote almost no time to finding the right mortgage. The assumption seems to be that all mortgages are created equal, when that's not true at all. Even a seemingly tiny difference in the interest rate can add or subtract tens of thousands of dollars to the financing cost of the home.

Which brings us to adjustable-rate mortgages. These mortgages can save a home buyer money, or even allow them to buy a more expensive house for the same monthly payment. Sometimes they can be the best decision a home buyer makes. In fact, between the two of us, we've had a total of six mortgages, and all have been ARMs. But we're firmly in the minority. Most of the time, ARMs are completely overlooked. ARMs won't be the right choice in all cases, of course, but at the very least, in our view, home buyers should take the time to find out whether they're the right choice in *their* case.

Why *are* ARMs so often ignored? For one thing, they didn't even hit the scene until 1982. That's when Congress passed the Garn–St. Germain Depository Institutions Act, making ARMs legal for the very first time.

They're also more complicated than a straightforward, fixed-rate mortgage. With a fixed-rate mortgage, you go to the bank, take out a loan for a sizeable percentage of the cost of the home (80 or 90 percent), and then agree to pay back that loan in set-amount, monthly installments at a guaranteed interest rate for the next three decades. The interest rate is set in stone. Historically, the interest rate can be lower than 3 percent or as high as 17 percent. It depends on what the rate is when you lock it in. Recently, it has

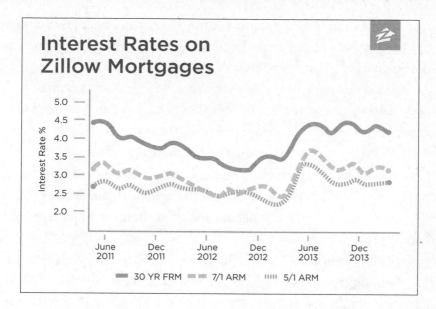

Interest Rates on Zillow Mortgages

Y-axis: Interest Rate %

X-axis: June 2011, Dec 2011, June 2012, Dec 2012, June 2013, Dec 2013

Legend: 30 YR FRM — 7/1 ARM — 5/1 ARM

been hovering just over 4 percent and is predicted to rise to 5 percent in the near future.

Adjustable-rate mortgages are a bit trickier. You take out a loan for the same percentage of the sale price, but repay the interest according to a variable scale. ARMs specify an initial interest rate term—often one, three, five, or seven years—during which the loan repayment is identical to an FRM. After the initial period is up, however, the interest rate and monthly payment adjusts each year according to an agreed-upon market index and margin for the remainder or the loan.

During the bubble, these kinds of loans were more popular than ever. As interest rates dropped in the 2000s, ARMs and other more complex mortgage products, such as interest-only loans, became much more prevalent. For some borrowers who flipped their houses before the sky fell, these ARMs worked out beautifully, saving them a lot of money because of the lower up-front rates. But ARMs got a bad rap when lenders began targeting riskier, "subprime" borrowers, plying them with deceptively low "teaser rates" that quickly led to sky-high rate increases of 5 percent or more. As housing prices dropped and interest rates rose, monthly payments increased and a lot of folks were unable to make these higher payments, resulting in foreclosure for many homeowners with ARMs.

But that doesn't mean ARMs are a bad deal for certain borrowers. In fact, our analysis shows that ARMs have been, and can remain, a good deal in certain circumstances.

Let's compare how two different families fared over time with these two different types of mortgages. We'll start in 1986, because that's when Freddie Mac started its Primary Mortgage Market Survey, which has historically been a major source for mortgage rate data.

In 1986, Fran and Robert Morgan—FRM, as their vanity plate reads—bought a $200,000 four-bedroom home in Orlando, Florida. They put 20 percent down, and took out a $160,000 thirty-year fixed-rate loan. Across the country, in Santa Fe, Susie and Norm Armstrong bought a three-bedroom condo that same year, for the exact same price and the same money down. But instead of an FRM, the Armstrongs opted for a 1/1 ARM (the only type of adjustable-rate mortgage available back then).

Because interest rates dropped from historic highs in the early 1980s, Susie and Norm's loan cost them $224,599 in monthly payments after fifteen years. Fran and Bob's thirty-year fixed cost $256,793 over the same time span. So, round one goes to the Armstrongs. Total out-of-pocket savings: $32,194 in saved interest.

There's another reason that the Armstrongs saved money in this scenario. In the first few years of a fixed-rate mortgage, you start accruing a sizeable amount of interest right off the bat, and you immediately have to start paying it down with your monthly payments. This costs extra cash in terms of interest payments over the life of the loan.

In contrast, ARMs have low interest rates in the early years. That means fewer financing costs that you eventually have to pay off in monthly payments over the life of the loan. In that way, taking out a loan with a lower interest rate initially can save you some serious money. Or, you can even use an ARM (with the same monthly payments as the FRM) to buy a more expensive house than you otherwise would have, while still paying the same overall out of-pocket expenditure in the end.

Of course, it won't always go this way. Remember, the ARM is a gamble. If interest rates don't go your way over the life of your mortgage, you won't save money at all. It's just one more factor to consider.

Let's imagine that the Armstrongs' daughter, Sabrina, is confronted with navigating this tricky guessing game when purchasing a new home. After searching on Zillow Mortgages, she learns that she can get either a thirty-year FRM at 5 percent interest or a conventional 5/1 ARM with an initial interest rate of 4.25 percent. Both loans require the same 20 percent down payment. Since the purchase price of Sabrina's new home is $200,000, her initial loan balance—regardless of which option she chooses—will be $160,000.

For the first five years, the FRM will cost Sabrina a total of $51,535 in monthly payments; the ARM, meanwhile, will cost $47,226. Clearly, the ARM is a better deal initially. For the first five years, Sabrina would save about $4,300 in interest and principal payments by choosing the ARM. Also, after five years, Sabrina's loan balance would be $146,926 for the FRM, versus $145,293 for the ARM. In other words, the ARM is paying off the loan slightly faster during the first five years, when the interest rate is .75 percent lower than that of the FRM.

But after five years, picking the better deal depends on two factors: luck (whether interest rates rise or fall) and planning (how long Sabrina plans to live in her home).

Let's consider the unluckiest of scenarios: Sabrina chooses an ARM, and interest rates skyrocket. In that case, if interest rates were to rise as fast as they possibly can, Sabrina's mortgage rate would adjust from 4.25 percent in year 5 to 9.25 percent in year 6, and remain there for the rest of her mortgage.

Sabrina's monthly payment would climb to $1,244 from $787, a $457 hike.* In this worst-case scenario, as soon as the end of year 6, the FRM would have been cheaper than the ARM. Ouch.

So, what should Sabrina do?

Again, it all depends on those two variables: planning and luck.

First and foremost, if Sabrina and her family are planning to live in their new home for five years or less and then put it on the market, then the ARM is definitely the way to go. But if they plan to stay for six years or longer, that's when Sabrina needs to look in the mirror and ask herself the same question that Clint Eastwood urged his assailant to ponder in the classic film *Dirty Harry*:

"Do (I) feel lucky?"

If the answer to that question is yes—in other words, if Sabrina thinks interest rates won't rise, and that, if they do, it'll be a modest amount and a long way off—then she should go with the ARM.

If she answers no, then she should either explore a longer-term ARM or an even longer-term fixed-rate mortgage.

We know what you're thinking. Who cares about imaginary Sabrina—what about *me*?

Well, depending on the initial rate spread and how long you plan to stay in your home, ARMs may well become cheaper yet again. The table on the next page shows how long a 7/1 ARM is cheaper than an FRM with a 5 percent interest rate, with various ARM interest rates. The table assumes that after the seventh year, the ARM interest rate rises 5 percent and remains there, a worst-case scenario for a conventional loan.

If you look at the table on the next page, you can see what happens to the spread between the FRM and the ARM when the interest rates move further apart. And as you can see, *the bigger the spread between the initial rate and the fixed rate, the longer the ARM will be the better deal.*

---

* Things would work out a little differently with an FHA loan or more moderate rise in interest rates. With an FHA ARM, the rate would rise 2 percent each year until it hits 10.25 percent and stays there.

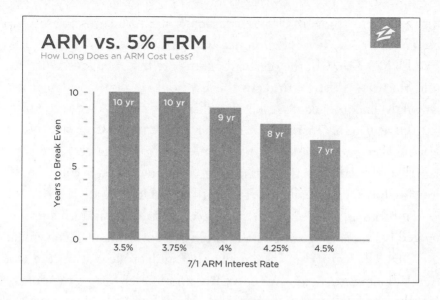

That said, it's impossible to be *100 percent* certain that an adjustable-rate mortgage is right for you. Since we can't predict the future, there will always be some element of risk involved. But instead of running from that risk, you should learn more about it. Don't just ask yourself if you're feeling lucky. Ask if you're feeling *informed.* Do some homework (we'll skip the shameless plug here) and find out what the odds are that taking that risk could bring you a substantial reward. You should do your homework and look at all the options on the table. After all, if you just blindly go with a fixed-rate mortgage, you could lose out in a very big way.

That's why we tend to agree with David Foster Wallace. "Let us in fact in our minds and hearts," he wrote, "say yes—*shout* yes—to the skirt, the kilt, the toga, the sarong, the jupe. Let us dream of or even in our spare time work toward an America where nobody lays any arbitrary sumptuary prescriptions on anyone else and we can all go around as comfortable and aerated and unchafed and unsquished and motile as we want."[8]

Mortgages, like pants, should be tailored to fit the person wearing them. And just as we should give some thought to the best way to cover our legs, we should also carefully consider our ARMs.

Because one thing is clear: Americans are over-utilizing FRMs when they could be saving money with ARMs.

As we've shown, the reasons for this are historical and cultural, but they're also structural. In the US housing market, buyers are strongly encouraged to take out thirty-year FRMs. Meanwhile, banks reasonably insist that the government underwrite the risk of giving home buyers a lower, fixed rate for a much longer time horizon. That means, for the vast majority of Americans, if you want to buy a house, you need a government-backed loan to do it.

Of course, one reason FRMs look so attractive in terms of low mortgage rates is because of the extensive government involvement described before. This system buckled and broke during the last housing downturn, and we currently find ourselves in a temporary fix in which the government owns the entities that back most of the mortgages in the United States right now.

This system must and will change. Some folks are working to reform it. We applaud their efforts and have tried to shine a spotlight on their work through housing forums put on by Zillow. A basic reality running through most of these reform proposals, however, is that shifting more responsibility and risk onto private lenders will result in somewhat higher rates on thirty-year fixed-rate mortgages than under the current system. This seems a reasonable trade-off to make in order to have a system that will work even when housing markets turn nasty. It will also start to make ARMs more attractive to a lot of borrowers, which is why our advice to you, dear reader, is as follows:

Sometimes an ARM will make more sense than an FRM.

Don't assume an FRM is the best choice for you just because conventional wisdom says, "that's how it's always been done." Determining your home loan is one of the most important financial decisions you'll ever make, and you owe it to yourself to do a little *home*work before buying a home.

Exterior of the Bates Hotel from the movie *Psycho (Paramount Pictures/ Photofest)*

8

Apples and Oranges

*How to Determine Whether Buying
a Foreclosure Is a Good Deal*

Apples and oranges. We all know the rule—you can't compare them. What does it matter that a certain apple is larger than a certain orange? What information can possibly be gleaned from the fact that a given orange is juicier than a given apple? They're completely different fruits! Comparing apples and oranges goes against centuries of axiomatic law. It just isn't done.

Except, that is, when it comes to real estate.

Conventional wisdom is rife with reports of the "foreclosure discount"—the savings associated with buying a bank-owned home. Talk to most real estate investors and they'll say that buyers can expect a significant reduction in price when purchasing a foreclosure. But in our post-bubble real estate market, which has been flooded with foreclosed homes, it's important that home buyers understand the *real* value proposition of foreclosures.

The fact is, while the foreclosure discount certainly exists, the traditional way of calculating it compares apples and oranges, producing a flawed valuation and distorting the actual savings buyers can hope to achieve. In this chapter we are going to tell you how to accurately compute the discount. It's often a lot less than the public has been led to believe.

To get to the core of the issue (pun intended), it's best to start at the beginning.

More than two-thirds of Americans finance their home purchase in some way. The system generally works well—unless the homeowner runs into trouble and can no longer afford to make his or her mortgage payments. Non-payment results in a default on the loan, and the bank assumes possession of the property. The bank then evicts the residents, takes control of the house, and sells it in order to recoup its loss on the loan.

This is a foreclosure—and it's not a pretty sight.

Unfortunately, it's something we've seen a whole lot of during the past few years, because failed mortgages were a contributing factor to the Great Recession, and also a consequence of it. Before the 2008 financial crisis, banks sought to capitalize on what was, at that point, a strong economy and an amped-up housing market. They offered more and more subprime mortgages—loans to families who, under normal circumstances, wouldn't qualify for a mortgage at all due to low credit scores or incomplete credit histories. It was a dangerous move because, despite the booming economy, these families had a higher risk of default.

In those years, a lot of people raised red flags about this dangerous practice. In 2006, I (Spencer) even wrote a blog post on Zillow called "The Tidal Wave is Coming": "A lot of homeowners who bought houses beyond their means a few years ago via low introductory rate ARMs are suddenly going to find themselves unable to pay their new higher mortgage," I wrote. "I'm worried about the impact that this will have on housing prices and more importantly on the overall American (and global?) economy."

This is one of those times I wish I had been wrong.

From an economic perspective, the foreclosure crisis was catastrophic for families, for banks (which are still short billions of dollars in loans that went bust), and for the economy at large. The bottom fell out from the housing market. Demand plummeted. When times are tough, no one is looking to buy. As a result, in

December 2009, new housing starts were at their lowest point since World War II.

Eventually, the worst of the storm cleared. In 2010, buyers started to emerge, and they were on the hunt for a good deal. Whether they were investors looking to take advantage of a down market, or families wanting to save some money on a home purchase, many buyers zeroed in on so-called "distressed homes" in order to capitalize on the much-rumored foreclosure discount.

These prospective buyers were lured with promises of massive savings. "Amazing deals!" "Foreclosures on the cheap!" A CNN article claimed, "Nationwide, the average discount on homes sold in a foreclosure was 39 percent below conventional sale prices." It went on to say that you could buy a home in Dayton, Ohio, for "57 percent below regular market prices."

If you think all of that sounds too good to be true, you're right. These traditional foreclosure discounts are based on a flawed calculation. To understand the nature of the flaw, let's first take a look at the very legitimate reasons why foreclosures generally do sell for less.

For one, foreclosures tend to be not as well maintained as non-foreclosures. After all, foreclosures are the result of financial distress on the part of the owner. Therefore, when the bank repossesses them, it's often discovered that certain home upkeep has been deferred. When money is tight, fixes to the roof, pipes, or water heater lose out to more essential purchases, like food, clothes, and gas.

Not only that, but when homeowners are evicted, it's not uncommon for them to take out their frustration on the home itself. They'll remove anything of value that can be resold. Plumbing fixtures, copper piping, and appliances are just a few of the items that some owners will take with them on their way out. When I (Spencer) bought a foreclosure in 2012, the house had been stripped of all its appliances, lightbulbs, and pretty much anything that could be taken from the house. And since the banks do not typically pay for extensive repairs on foreclosed homes, these deficiencies then become factored into the price of foreclosed homes when banks put them back on the market.

Banks also drive the foreclosure discount in another way. They want foreclosed homes off their books as quickly as possible. Therefore, they aren't going to act like a traditional home seller, patiently comparing offers in order to find the one that makes the most financial sense. Banks are in the business of lending to consumers to buy homes—not owning homes themselves. Therefore, their goal is simply to unload foreclosed properties fast, which leads to cheaper prices on the open market. The bank wants to sell as quickly as possible, and the buyer leverages that fact to push for a good deal on the foreclosed property.

Foreclosures also tend to be cheaper because of the inherent risk involved in purchasing them. Banks aren't required to disclose the same information that a private seller would, and they don't necessarily allow buyers to conduct an inspection of the property. If the home is bought at an auction, potential buyers are essentially bidding on it as-is and sight unseen. Naturally, this results in knocking at least a few percentage points off the price. Finally, buyers tend to expect a foreclosure discount because there is a stigma attached to these homes.

For all of the reasons above, foreclosures are generally seen as being inferior, or problematic, even if the specific foreclosure in question is not. Given all of these contributing factors, it's no wonder that the foreclosure discount is thought to be so extraordinarily high.

But it isn't—or, at least, it hasn't been since the very worst part of the housing crisis.

Here's an example. In Pleasantville, let's say the median sale price for a home is $150,000. The median sale price for a foreclosed home is $100,000: ($100,000-$150,000)/$150,000 comes out to -33 percent. What a deal!

The math seems to make sense, but the logic of the calculation has a fatal flaw. By comparing foreclosed homes to non-foreclosed homes, the traditional equation assumes they are the same—that the houses are comparable in size, but not condition. In other words, it assumes that only the financial circumstances of one of the owners has changed. According to our data, however, the average foreclosure property is different from the average non-foreclosure.

Let's take a look at the city of Detroit, for instance. In June 2012, the median value of a foreclosed home was $47,000. Meanwhile the median value of a non-foreclosed home was $113,000. Using the traditional calculation we described, we might think the foreclosure discount in Detroit is a whopping 59 percent. Whoa! Where do I sign?

But this calculation doesn't take into account the material differences between the average foreclosure and the average non-foreclosure. The median non-foreclosure in Detroit has three bedrooms, two bathrooms, and boasts 1,700 square feet. The median foreclosure in Detroit, however, is a three-bed, one-bath that has only 1,200 square feet. In other words, the median non-foreclosed home has 500 extra square feet and an additional bathroom.

No wonder the non-foreclosed home was listed for significantly more than the foreclosed home. It's significantly bigger!

And therein lies the problem with the traditional foreclosure discount: It compares apples and oranges. The difference between the list price of the average foreclosure and non-foreclosure might be eye-popping, but it's also irrelevant. They're completely different fruits!

HOW TO CALCULATE THE REAL FORECLOSURE DISCOUNT

In order to get an accurate picture of the *real* foreclosure discount, we need to compare the average foreclosed home to similar properties that haven't been foreclosed on—a bruised apples to apples comparison, if you will. We can then compare the sale prices of the average foreclosure and similar non-foreclosures with their estimated home values to determine the extent to which foreclosures are *actually* discounted. In fact, we can even analyze historical data to see how foreclosed homes have fared relative to non-distressed properties over time.

In fairness to investors and real estate reporters, who up until now have propagated the myth of the massive foreclosure discount, this bruised apples to apples comparison is only possible if you know the fair market value of every single individual home, foreclosure and non-foreclosure alike.

That being said, using estimated home values to calculate the real foreclosure discount—we'll call it the RFD for short—shows how much the old calculation exaggerated the potential savings for buyers.

In fact, when we plug in the estimated home values and analyze the RFD, we find that the actual amount a buyer saved when purchasing a foreclosed home in September 2012 was only 7.7 percent! That's a far cry from the 25 to 35 percent often cited. At the height of the recession, the actual foreclosure discount *was* fairly close to what the conventional wisdom suggests. In September 2009, the RFD peaked at 23.7 percent. Since then, however, it's been on a steady downward track.

When we ran the numbers, we found that between January 2004 and September 2012, the RFD fluctuated every month somewhere between 7.7 percent and 23.7 percent. Remember, though, that this is the national range. When we dig into foreclosures on the local level, the reality behind the tale of the foreclosure discount becomes even more complicated.

Foreclosure Discount Over Time

Real Foreclosure Discount =
Discount Based on Median Sale Price =

As you might expect, some regional housing markets see higher discounts than the national average. Others see lower ones. But in still other markets, there is virtually no foreclosure discount all.

How can we explain that?

This is where the laws of economics come into play. In markets with high housing demand, it apparently doesn't matter if a home is a foreclosure or not. With plenty of willing buyers, there is no financial incentive for a bank to price a foreclosure below market value, and buyers aren't able to get away with lower offers just because the property was foreclosed on.

You don't need a discount to entice someone to move on a home in South Beach, or Southern California, for instance. Miami's discount is a scant 2.9 percent. In sunny San Diego, the RFD is only 2.4 percent.

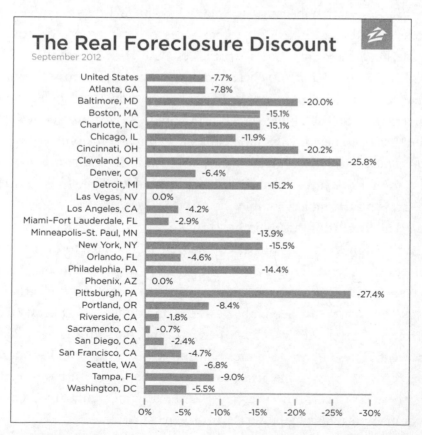

The Real Foreclosure Discount
September 2012

United States	-7.7%
Atlanta, GA	-7.8%
Baltimore, MD	-20.0%
Boston, MA	-15.1%
Charlotte, NC	-15.1%
Chicago, IL	-11.9%
Cincinnati, OH	-20.2%
Cleveland, OH	-25.8%
Denver, CO	-6.4%
Detroit, MI	-15.2%
Las Vegas, NV	0.0%
Los Angeles, CA	-4.2%
Miami–Fort Lauderdale, FL	-2.9%
Minneapolis–St. Paul, MN	-13.9%
New York, NY	-15.5%
Orlando, FL	-4.6%
Philadelphia, PA	-14.4%
Phoenix, AZ	0.0%
Pittsburgh, PA	-27.4%
Portland, OR	-8.4%
Riverside, CA	-1.8%
Sacramento, CA	-0.7%
San Diego, CA	-2.4%
San Francisco, CA	-4.7%
Seattle, WA	-6.8%
Tampa, FL	-9.0%
Washington, DC	-5.5%

On the flip side, some markets, like Las Vegas or Phoenix, have no foreclosure discount precisely because they were hit so hard by the recession. In these cities, and others like them, the market is so full of bank-owned homes—as high as 50 percent of all homes on the market, in some cases—that there is just nothing taboo about them. Rather than being separated from the normal pool of available homes, they are fully integrated—a fact that is reflected in their sale prices.

In other locales, the price of a foreclosure and a non-foreclosure become functionally the same for the very opposite reason—because there aren't many houses on the market at all. When the supply drops like this, bank-owned homes become more valuable to potential buyers, simply because there are fewer options for buyers to consider. In other words, economics kicks in: Low supply leads to higher prices.

This situation became especially prevalent after the housing market collapsed in 2007. Home prices dropped sharply nation-wide, making many homes worth less than their mortgages. (We call this "negative equity.") Homeowners were loath to sell, since they knew they wouldn't make back enough money to pay off their mortgages. So they hung on to their homes—and thus the market had fewer homes of any kind available to buy. Home builders were cautious about new developments, too, because of the down real estate market. Just by virtue of being available, then, foreclosures became a little more valuable.

The flipside of this dynamic is that areas with low demand will see the highest foreclosure discounts. All sellers have to drop their prices sharply to entice people to buy at all, and that includes the sellers of distressed properties—banks. We see this most clearly in Rust Belt cities. In September 2012, Cincinnati's RFD was 20.2 percent, Cleveland's was 25.8 percent, and Pittsburgh's was 27.4 percent. These figures are more in line with conventional wisdom based on the flawed means of calculating the foreclosure discount. In these instances, however, buyers are really and truly able to find significant savings by purchasing a foreclosure.

There's one more reason that the foreclosure discount tends to be lower than people imagine: The practice of buying a foreclosure has become much more common since the recession began. In early 2014, approximately 10 percent of home sales were formerly fore-closed properties, compared to the pre-2006 average of less than 2 percent.

As the stigma slowly washes away, discounts are much less nec-essary to convince people to buy these distressed properties. When you see your friends doing it, maybe you'll consider doing it, too.

Nevertheless, even as the stigma diminishes, the misinformation about the foreclosure discount is as widespread as ever. You hear it from home buyers convinced they're about to find their dream home for half off. And you hear it in the dire warnings of policy makers, politicians, and reporters.

When the foreclosure discount reached a peak in the middle of the housing crisis, there was much consternation about a poten-tial flood of massively underpriced homes entering the market and driving home prices down nationwide. The concern was that non-distressed homeowners—the ones who were dutiful about paying their mortgages and who weren't underwater—would be left high and dry as buyers flocked to the bargain-bin foreclosures.

At the time, these fears had some basis. But now, when you look at the data, it's clear that people don't need to fear future foreclo-sures in the same way. Going forward, foreclosed homes just won't be cheap enough to drive down prices across the country. The mod-est discount that *does* exist is already baked into the housing market.

We know the housing market, like the produce aisle, can be a confusing place. With apples and oranges—not to mention Asian pears, star fruit, kumquats, and the like—it can be hard to make sense of it all. No wonder generations of buyers and sellers have relied on flawed comparisons that fueled the foreclosure discount myth.

But now, we don't have to settle for simple but misleading approximations anymore. We can stack the apples alongside the apples, bruised though they may be, and make a smart pick.

Exterior of Bluth model home in Sudden Valley from the TV show *Arrested Development* (Fox Network/Photofest)

9

What to Expect When You're Inspecting

How to Pick the Right Home Inspector

It's the stuff of nightmares. You've spent countless hours scouring listings. You've gone to more open houses than you can remember. You've emailed your real estate agent more often than your own darn mother. But after months of narrowing your options, you finally found it—the perfect home.

Or, at least, it *seemed* like the perfect home.

Once you moved in, problems began emerging from underneath the floorboards, between the walls, and practically everywhere else. The chimney crown is cracked, part of the roof decking is rotting, the septic tank leaks. Had your home inspector caught these issues, you could have estimated the cost of the repairs, reevaluated the price of the house, and either negotiated with the seller or walked away. Instead, you're stuck with a massive headache and a large repair bill.

As frightening as it sounds, this scenario isn't far-fetched. In fact, it's a story we've heard countless times via social media.

For Christine, her inspector's damage estimate on cracks in the house's foundation woefully undersold the extent of necessary repairs—to the tune of $16,000—and made no mention of the leaking pipes on the second floor.

Megan's inspector missed broken water shutoff valves, leaks, and a bulging hot water tank. Like many of us, she might not even have been aware that water tanks *could* bulge—but it's the kind of damage that proves to be expensive and extremely dangerous.

In Robin's case, the inspector didn't spot a hole in the roof! As a consolation for the oversight, her inspector offered to re-inspect the house, though after she had already closed. Talk about a day late and dollar short.

For millions of Americans, once you've laid eyes on "the One," you just want to get the paperwork over with, and start hanging up the flat-screen. But for all the attention and effort that prospective home buyers put into their search, far too many neglect a critical final step to ensuring their residential bliss: finding a reliable home inspector.

In some cases, however, the person judging the quality of your massive new investment may be little more than the cable guy moonlighting as a home inspector. And this short-sightedness can leave you saddled with massive costs from issues that went unnoticed.

Luckily, it's a mistake you can avoid with ease. All you need to do is put in a little time finding a respected and dependable home inspector. And we've developed several simple guidelines to help you inspect your inspector.

First, *do your homework.*

As you go about your search, check to see how long your potential inspectors have been in the business, how qualified and experienced they are, and whether or not they're licensed, bonded, and insured. Be skeptical of how they present themselves and ask for clarification if something seems ambiguous—for example, ten years of industry experience is not the same as ten years as a home inspector.

Client testimonials are a great way to infer the quality of service you can expect from a home inspector. At Zillow, we offer our own professional directory with listings and ratings for local home inspectors. Online databases like Angie's List also offer ratings and reviews for home inspectors in your area. If you're hiring the services of a firm, make sure the reviews indicate a consistent level of quality for all of the inspectors employed. The more reviews there are, the more you can trust what you read. And don't be shy about asking a home inspector for references from previous customers.

Second, *try before you buy.*

Ask the home inspectors you are considering for sample reports. Ideally, you want to read a report on a good house, and—importantly—one on a problematic house, too. Good inspectors will have these on hand, and the best will have them featured front and center on their website.

When reading these reports, keep in mind what a home inspection does and doesn't cover. For example, home inspectors typically don't perform tests for radon or mold, inspect for termites, or check the soil. You can ask an inspector for advice on additional investigations, and they might be able to recommend the best course of action and trusted vendors. Ultimately, though, it's up to you to decide whether or not to seek further inspections.

Take note of the language used in the sample reports. A good home inspection report will clearly state the problem, explain its significance if it's not obvious, and recommend a course of action. Reports that suggest additional inspections should raise some eyebrows. Because additional inspections cost time and money, good home inspectors will not make these recommendations unless they are needed—otherwise, they may be written specifically to cover the hide of the home inspector.

Third, *first impressions matter.*

Pay attention to how home inspectors present themselves. You want someone who clearly cares about his or her reputation, is easily reachable, and is professional from the start. A website under construction is a red flag. Unresponsiveness to calls or emails is another warning sign, as are inconsistent ratings. Any one of these should give you pause, but a combination means you should continue your search.

Of course, the process doesn't end with choosing an inspector.

No matter how much you trust your well-vetted inspector, make sure to attend the inspection itself. A good inspector will provide detailed notes in their report, with feedback on maintenance options, but some things are going to be easier to understand in person. Ask your inspector to point things out to you as you walk the property, so that you have a better understanding of any underlying issues.

Whenever possible, follow your inspector wherever they go—whether it's onto the roof, into the basement, or down the crawl-spaces. They should note things that you need to be aware of calmly and impartially. Also, bring a friend or family member along if you can. With such a big investment on the line, an extra set of eyes can't hurt.

Finding the perfect house is hard. Once you do, you should make sure it is perfect by hiring a trusted home inspector.

MOVING OUT

THE NEW RULES OF SELLING A HOME

The Ingalls family in front of their home from the show *Little House on the Prairie (NBC/Photofest)*

America's Next Top Remodel

Not All Home-Improvement Projects Are Created Equal

Home improvement," Harvard University's Joint Center on Housing Studies astutely observed, "has become the great national pastime."[1] Despite a serious dip during the Great Recession, US spending on residential renovations was on the rise again, approaching about $125 billion in 2012.[2]

We engage in this passionate pastime for a lot of reasons, of course. Because Junior needs a playroom. Because the kitchen hasn't been updated since the Cold War. Because three kids and one bathroom feels downright primitive.

But many of us share *another* major motivation to spruce up the powder room or install gleaming new appliances: a desire to increase the resale value of our home.

I (Spencer) saw this firsthand, when my in-laws listed their Burbank, California, home for sale at $475,000. After receiving just a few offers from investors—a sign that there wasn't much demand for their home—they decided to do some remodeling in hopes of increasing the desirability of the property, and driving up their asking price, too. Fast-forward about six months and about $50,000 in home improvements, and my in-laws quickly found a family who paid $575,000 for the remodeled home. In other words, they doubled the money invested in sprucing up the house.

That's the scenario most everyone has in mind when making home improvements. We instinctively believe that making our home nicer will boost the value of our property. We're convinced that any and all improvements will "pay for themselves" when it comes time to sell. We assume that expensive and time-consuming upgrades are "worth more" than smaller upgrades. It certainly worked out great for my in-laws—but, as it turns out, not all home improvements are created equal.

To determine which bangs of the hammer give you the greatest bang for your buck, we compared thousands of pairs of home values across a wide spectrum of home improvements. This allowed us to zero in on the impact of individual renovations and determine, *on average*, how much a particular improvement increases the resale value of a home.

In our analysis, we investigated nine types of home improvements, from upscale kitchen renovations, to the addition of a story, to renovating a basement. As expected, each and every improvement *did* indeed increase the value of a home. But the level of increase varied in some unexpected ways. It turns out that certain improvements will increase a home's value by *more* than the cost of the renovation. Meanwhile, other improvements actually add *less* value than the cost of the renovation.

THE LAW OF DIMINISHING RETURNS

We were surprised to find that spending a lot more money on a home renovation doesn't necessarily increase the resale value more than spending a lot less money.

How does this play out in practice? Let's say you bought your home when you were on a budget, and now that you find yourself in more comfortable circumstances, you want to upgrade your run-down bathroom. Based on our analysis, a $3,000 mid-range bathroom remodel—for instance, replacing the toilet and light fixtures, adding a double sink, and installing some wallpaper—would result in a $1.71 increase in home value for every $1.00 you spent on the renovation.

That's a pretty sweet deal. So why stop there? Why not go even further and transform your bathroom into a porcelain palace, complete with partitioned toilets, fancy jet massage showerheads, and humidistat-controlled exhaust fans?

Well, it turns out (again, on average) that plunking down $12,000 to upgrade to an upscale bathroom results only in a $0.87 increase in home value for every dollar you spend. Your home value would still increase, of course, but you wouldn't recover the full cost of the renovation.

The same goes for another common home improvement: windows. On average, a homeowner will recover $1.15 for every $1.00 she spends installing new mid-range windows. But if you choose to turn your home into the Sistine Chapel and install beautiful, double-glazed windows with some lovely stained hardwood interior trim, you'll most likely break even at $1.01 recouped in increased home value for every $1.00 spent.

It may seem counterintuitive that these upscale improvements return less than mid-range renovations. After all, if spending some money on a renovation is good, then shouldn't spending more money on a renovation be better?

We think the reason has to do with function versus fashion, and a little thing that economists call "diminishing returns."

Take a bathroom that's in pretty bad shape—dripping sink, busted mirror, broken toilet, and a shower that won't turn on. Restoring this bathroom to a serviceable state, a mid-range renovation, should increase the value of a home significantly, since it completely changes the livability of the property. In contrast, taking a fully functional bathroom and turning it into Donald Trump's luxury bathroom with gold-plated, monogrammed toilet flushers doesn't do much to change the usability of the room.

The same goes for window renovations. A mid-range upgrade

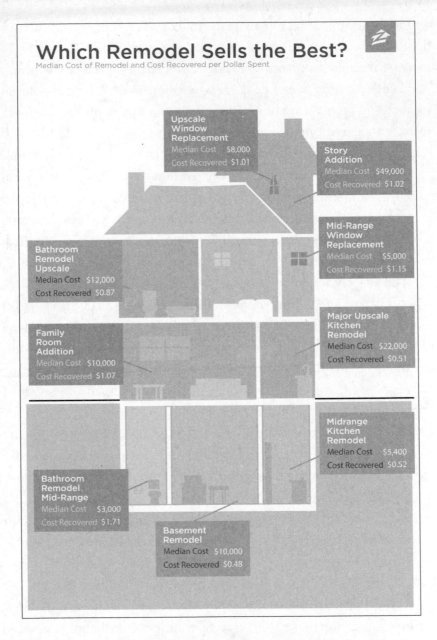

Which Remodel Sells the Best?
Median Cost of Remodel and Cost Recovered per Dollar Spent

Upscale Window Replacement
Median Cost $8,000
Cost Recovered $1.01

Story Addition
Median Cost $49,000
Cost Recovered $1.02

Mid-Range Window Replacement
Median Cost $5,000
Cost Recovered $1.15

Bathroom Remodel Upscale
Median Cost $12,000
Cost Recovered $0.87

Major Upscale Kitchen Remodel
Median Cost $22,000
Cost Recovered $0.51

Family Room Addition
Median Cost $10,000
Cost Recovered $1.07

Midrange Kitchen Remodel
Median Cost $5,400
Cost Recovered $0.52

Bathroom Remodel Mid-Range
Median Cost $3,000
Cost Recovered $1.71

Basement Remodel
Median Cost $10,000
Cost Recovered $0.48

likely improves the functionality of the windows—maybe keeping out the cold better and saving a bit on your heating bill—but has little amenity value. An upscale window renovation, however, doesn't make the windows work any better—they just look nicer. As a result, it doesn't increase the value of the home as significantly.

THE KITCHEN SINK

Here's something else to keep in mind before you *sink* a lot of money into a brand-new kitchen: Kitchen renovations, at any level, offer among *the lowest* return on investment of the home improvements we studied. Yes, you read that correctly.

For a mid-range kitchen remodel, the typical family spends $5,400. Meanwhile, a major upscale kitchen renovation can cost you over four times as much, at $22,000. Yet if you look at the chart, both upscale and mid-range kitchen renovations recover about half the cost invested. Every dollar you spend on a new kitchen only increases the value of your home by 50 cents—regardless of how much the renovation costs.

So if you're planning a kitchen renovation, the most important consideration is the functionality you're hoping to achieve when you're cooking dinner—not the value you're trying to create when it comes time to put your home on the market.

AIM HIGH

We also investigated the return-on-investment for adding a story versus renovating a basement.

Given that remodeling a basement tends to cost around $10,000, while adding a second or third story can reach five times that amount, a basement might seem the way to go. Except that, at $1.02 per $1.00 spent, a story addition lets you recoup the full cost of the remodel. A basement renovation, on the other hand, only returns $0.48 cents on the dollar, the lowest ROI of any of the nine home improvements we analyzed.

It's hard to say exactly why this is the case. Maybe it's because, when you add a story, it immediately increases the curb appeal of your home, making it appear instantly bigger, grander, and thus more valuable to passers-by. Or maybe it's the lack of natural light in the basement, or the general feeling—even if you've added a

20-by-30-foot entertaining area with a wet bar and a bathroom—
that basements are dank, prone to flooding, and usually where a
movie's psycho killer stores the bodies.

Or, more likely, while both add usable space to your home, only
one adds square footage you didn't have before. And thus, maybe it
shouldn't be surprising that only adding a story also adds value to
your home equity.

CAVEAT, BUILDER

These are important trends to keep in mind when considering how
to allocate your renovation budget. But also keep in mind that they
don't factor depreciation into the equation.

Just as a car loses value over time (even as soon as you drive
it off the lot), it's natural to expect that home renovations will
decrease in value the older they are. The simple fact is that even a
state-of-the-art Sub-Zero refrigerator will be dated after a decade
or two. Our research shows that, each and every year, you lose
about $2,600 of the incremental resale potential attributable to
a remodel. That means that if you spent $5,000 on a mid-range
bathroom remodel, $8,000 on new upscale windows, and $16,000
renovating your basement, you can expect your home's resale value
to increase by $24,310. Just one year later, however, you'll capture
less than $22,000 of that benefit.

Another thing to consider is that these results reflect national
averages, not the local real estate market in your neighborhood.
These are the trends we've identified by scouring the data everywhere from Manhattan condos to Midwestern ranch homes. And
while we've included the basic parameters of our categories, the
definition of "upscale" varies significantly; one homeowner's upscale
could be another's piddling mid-range remodel.

What that means is that results for specific projects may vary
considerably. One family might lose $0.52 per dollar on their
basement remodel, and another homeowner might gain $0.30 per

dollar spent on their dream basement rehab. As they say in those late-night ads for over-the-counter medical products: "Individual results may vary."

Finally, it bears repeating that practically *all* home renovations increase a home's value to *some* extent. Moreover, we can't put a dollar figure on how much a family will enjoy any particular improvement. For you, the renovation may be worth the cost independent of any increase in your home value. So don't let these relative return-on-investment statistics stop you from building that rumpus room you've always wanted, or the basement wine cave of your dreams. Generally speaking, renovating your home *will* boost your property value.

Nevertheless, if you're trying to *maximize* that added value, a mid-range bathroom remodel will certainly give you the most bang for your buck. Beyond that, the choice is up to you—though we do think that this book would look rather nice on a mahogany bookshelf in a newly redecorated family room. Just saying.

Exterior of the Simpsons' home from the TV show *The Simpsons (Fox Network/ Photofest)*

Magic Words and Dangerous Descriptors
How to Write an Effective Listing

As she recounted it in the *Wall Street Journal* (and more recently in a book), digital strategist Amy Webb could pinpoint the exact moment when she realized that she needed a new approach to online dating. It was when one of her online dates turned out to be married. And it led to an epiphany: *Her profile was attracting the wrong kind of man.* The solution, she decided, was to apply her professional skills to help strengthen her online dating presence.

Amy sprang into action. First, she created ten fake profiles of male archetypes, giving them usernames like JewishDoc1000. Then, she sat back and watched as women started contacting her fake profiles, mining the interactions to answer several key questions about her competition: What were the women who had more popular profiles saying and doing? What words did they use to describe themselves? About what did they fib? How long were their profiles? How and when did they initiate contact?

During the month Amy operated her ten fake male profiles, she interacted with ninety-six women. She analyzed what worked and what didn't. By the end of her research, she had all the information she needed to "reverse engineer" her own perfect online profile.

Amy's story has a fairy-tale ending. One of the men who responded to her new profile ended up being The One. And these days, the only married man she goes on dates with is her husband, Brian.[1]

Zillow isn't getting into the dating game. But we've certainly seen our share of missed connections between home buyers and sellers. We know how frustrating it can be to search endlessly for The One.

So, like Amy, we decided to mine the data—and to see if we could build a better *house*-trap. Across 24,000 home sales, we measured how different words, descriptions, and listing lengths impacted sale prices of homes. And we learned the same thing that Amy did. When it comes to real estate listings, words matter. And if you're not careful, picking the wrong adjective could cost you time, money, and in some cases, lots of both.

One example makes the case. Just look, for instance, at the word "unique." You might think being unique is a good thing. It's certainly an attribute when you're advertising yourself to potential partners on an online dating site. Well, when we ran the numbers, we found out that if a house is described as "unique" it can sell for as much as 30 to 50 percent *less* than expected!

Why the enormous drop? Because our database shows that homes described as "unique" tend to need work or some kind of rehab. If a home is described as a "unique opportunity," for instance, that's a negative signal, whether or not the seller is trying to send one.

And that's not the only word that can give buyers the wrong impression. To understand just how powerful your language can be, consider this hypothetical listing:

> If you're looking for a unique, modern home, we've got the house for you! Complete with a gourmet kitchen and hardwood floors throughout, this quaint home has the potential to be your dream house. Located on a picturesque cul-de-sac, this house is part of a very nice neighborhood— and a great investment for any home buyer.

Sounds pretty good, right? But based on our data, the odds are that there are some hidden messages buried in those words. Here's a translation of what this ad is *really* saying to prospective buyers:

> We're really grasping for something good to tell you about this home and its features. It was built over half a century ago, and it's quite small at 1,299 square feet. This place needs a lot of work. And, honestly, there's nothing special about the location.

How do we know that what seems like a perfectly fine listing is actually communicating price-threatening messages to potential buyers? Well, because the Zillow database tells us the truth behind common euphemisms used in home listings. And once you, too, know what to look for, you'll also be able to spot the hidden messages.

DON'T LIE ABOUT YOUR HOME'S AGE

In the same way that sellers use the word "unique" to sugarcoat the less desirable aspects of their homes, there's a similar dynamic at work with the word "modern," though depending on your taste it can be a big boon. You might think that a "modern home" was built fairly recently. After all, look up the word "modern," and Merriam-Webster's defines it as something "of, relating to, or characteristic of the present or the immediate past." But actually, the word "modern" tends to indicate that a home was built in the 1950s or 1960s. Many homes built during this period are known as Mid-Century Modern, an architectural style sought after by many home buyers, and especially common in areas like Palm Springs, California.

In fact, using data from past listings, we can venture a strong guess about when a home was built, just based on the adjective used to describe it. Again, the numbers tell the story. If you line up listings that use age-describing words like "modern" with the construction dates of the homes they characterize, you can see clear trends. Here's a helpful visual.

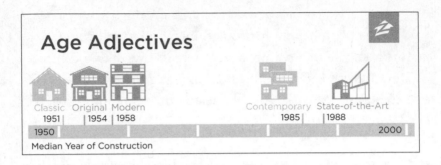

What's more, we found that *original* homes are even older than the so-called modern ones. And *classic* homes are classic in the same way that the movie *Gone with the Wind* is classic—which is to say, many date to the 1930s.

Obviously, words like "antique" and "rustic" imply that a house is on the older side. But even words like "traditional," "timeless," and "well-maintained" indicate older homes, according to our analysis. These words could indicate homes that are built in sought-after older styles such as traditional Craftsman or Colonial.

That said, we did find a few words that do signal recent construction and design: "state-of-the-art" and "contemporary." If you read one of those words, it's most likely that the home was built in the mid-to-late 1980s.

CHARMING EQUALS TEENY, AND OTHER CODE WORDS

Words like "cozy," "charming," "cute," and "quaint" are just as loaded with hidden meanings. Taken at face value, these words might not seem to convey anything concrete about a house. But in reality, they can reveal how large—or, in most cases, how small—a home probably is. When we crunched the numbers, we found that most sellers listing a small home will mask its true dimensions in these pleasant-sounding euphemisms.

Sure, the dictionary definition of cozy is "providing physical comfort." But in real estate jargon, it essentially means that you can expect a house to be so small your knees will brush the wall when you sit on the toilet.

Homes described as "charming" (on average 1,487 square feet), tend to be larger than homes described as "quaint" (1,299 square feet), and both are larger than homes described as "cute" (1,128 square feet). All of them are substantially smaller than the 1,640 square foot median-sized home in the universe we examined.

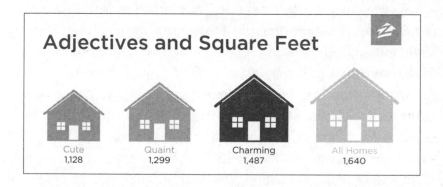

So let's return to our hypothetical listing. This is how we knew that it was a small home, and probably only about 1,299 square feet. The seller called it "quaint," and that gave it away.

But how did we know that the hypothetical house needed work? There were two dead giveaways. First, they told us it had a lot of *potential*. Then they claimed it was a great *investment*. Both words tend to mean that the home in question has seen better days. Or maybe it's a total dump.

Don't even get us started on what it means when a seller says a house just needs "a little TLC." In that case, you may as well pull up to your new home with a dump truck and a backhoe along with your moving van.

WORDS AREN'T SO CHEAP AFTER ALL

Some of this might sound intuitive, but these words aren't just abstract indicators. They can have a tangible impact on price, for better or for worse. They can add up to thousands of dollars in your pocket—or thousands that you might as well toss in the trash.

In eight thousand top-tier listings, we compared final sale prices of homes to their estimated values. And we saw a clear price drop in the final sale price—as much as almost 7 percent—just when the listing used "investment," "potential," or "TLC."

On the other end of the spectrum, word choice is just as important for a seller to consider. Bottom tier homes described as *luxurious* tend to beat their expected sale price by a whopping 8.2 percent. Top tier homes described as *captivating* tend to beat theirs by 6.5 percent. That means, if your home's estimated home value is $110,000, but your listing includes the key word "luxurious," you could pocket an extra $8,965. (Remember, however, that you'd better have the luxurious features to back that adjective up. The word alone doesn't get you the money. The reality it advertises does. We'll have more to say about that later.)

We also found something else that was interesting when we looked at the effect of the word "fantastic." One of our favorite books, Steven D. Levitt and Stephen J. Dubner's *Freakonomics*, argues that "fantastic" is a "dangerously ambiguous adjective." It essentially operates, they write, as "real-estate agent code for a house that doesn't have any specific attributes worth describing."[2]

With all due respect to the *Freakonomics* duo, however, we didn't find that to be the case. In fact, according to our data, the word "fantastic" often corresponds to a measurable bump in final sale prices of 2.8 percent. That's likely because the word tends to be used as an adjective that describes not just the house itself, but specific features within it—for instance, "fantastic views."

Across the board, this much is clear: *Words matter—and, most of all, they matter to your pocketbook*. We've all heard the old adage, "a picture is worth a thousand words." Well, when it comes to real estate listings, it turns out that the picture you're painting with certain words can be worth *thousands of dollars*.

Just look at the table below, which quantifies the effect that some of the most common descriptive words had on final prices when compared to expected values.

Decoding Listing Descriptions

Keyword	Bottom Tier $	Middle Tier $$	Top Tier $$$
Bargain	—	-3.5%	—
Basketball	4.5%	—	—
Beautiful	2.3%	—	—
Captivating	—	—	6.5%
Cosmetic	—	-2.5%	-7.5%
Custom	—	—	0.7%
Exquisite	—	1.9%	—
Fixer	—	-11.1%	—
Gentle	—	—	2.3%
Granite	4.2%	2.7%	1.1%
Impeccable	5.9%	—	—
Investment	-6.6%	—	—
Investor	-5.3%	—	-6.6%
Landscaped	4.2%	1.5%	1.6%
Luxurious	8.1%	—	—
Nice	-1.1%	-1.0%	—
Opportunity	-2.0%	—	—
Pergola	—	4.0%	—
Potential	-4.3%	—	—
Remodel	2.9%	1.8%	1.7%
Spotless	2.0%	—	—
Stainless	5.0%	2.8%	1.4%
Tile	2.0%	—	—
TLC	-4.2%	—	-8.7%
Updated	—	0.8%	—
Upgraded	1.8%	—	—

If you're listing your house, it's obvious that you should avoid words like "cosmetic," "bargain," and, especially, "fixer." But apparently just about everyone likes an *impeccable, gentle, remodeled* house. If you're wondering what the word "gentle" refers to, it commonly appears in listings as part of the phrase "gentle rolling hills."

Let's say you don't have something nice to say, though. Can you just say the house is, well, "nice"? Well, you *can*, but you shouldn't. Because if you can't say anything better than "nice" about your home, that probably means it's not, and the sale price will probably drop lower than expected in that case, too.

"LUXURY" SHACKS AND THE IMPORTANCE OF HONESTY

There is, however, one important caveat when considering the words you should use to list if you're selling, or the ones to look for if you're buying. It's important to remember that, in all of these cases, what's driving the increase in sale price isn't necessarily the adjective itself, but an underlying truth about the home.

A well-chosen adjective can certainly attract more visitors to your open house. More visitors might mean more competition, which might mean a bidding war, which might mean a higher final sale price. But that won't work if all those visitors who show up see a home that looks nothing like what the listing described.

So you can't drive up the price of your ramshackle hut next to the town dump just by calling it "an impeccably luxurious remodeled charmer" in the listing. Install wall-to-wall carpets made of ermine in every room, though, and you might be in business.

Just like you learned in elementary school, lying doesn't pay. But if you've got something nice to say, you should probably say it. (Just make sure not to use the *word* "nice"!)

In fact, the data shows that it can actually be a big mistake not to mention a potential selling point for your home.

Want an example? Let's talk about granite, for instance.

In 2011 to 2012, top-tier homes with "granite features" mentioned in the listing sold for 1.1 percent more than similar homes without "granite" in the listing. This effect becomes even more prominent in middle-tier homes (2.7 percent higher) and larger still in bottom-tier homes (4.16 percent).

Maybe homes with granite features are better maintained by the owners. Maybe if sellers fail to cite granite in the listing, they get fewer visits, reducing the competition to buy the home. Either way, the granite effect is clear.

Furthermore, we also found that the more objective quality words that appear in a listing—words like "granite," "landscaped," and "stainless"—the higher the home's final sale price tends to be.

This is because these words help make buyers aware of extra amenities that might not have been noticed in the listing photos. Put another way, they give you clues that really hint at the home's underlying value.

The lesson for sellers here is clear: If you've got it, flaunt it. Don't be shy. Don't be the guy with the granite countertops and landscaped backyard who sells his house for less just because he was too bashful to mention them in his listing.

THE LONGER THE LISTING, THE BIGGER THE SALES PRICE

If you're worrying about boring potential buyers, don't. *We've found that longer listings consistently sell for more.* Buyers want to know details, and those extra words can give them additional information about whether a house is worth the trek to see it in person. And, in doing so, they can often increase a home's final sale price.

As you can see from the following graph, homes listed with more words are much more likely to sell above their expected price. That's true whether a home is a million dollar mansion or a low cost fixer-upper.

You also can see here that more expensive homes tend to come with longer listings. That makes sense because there's simply more to say about bigger, fancier homes. They have more noteworthy features, and it takes more words to describe all those traits in a

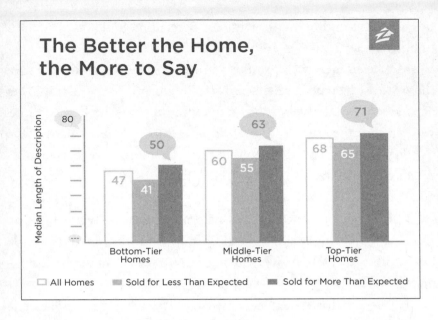

The Better the Home, the More to Say

Median Length of Description

| Bottom-Tier Homes | Middle-Tier Homes | Top-Tier Homes |

47 · 41 · 50 | 60 · 55 · 63 | 68 · 65 · 71

☐ All Homes   ■ Sold for Less Than Expected   ■ Sold for More Than Expected

home listing. So it's no surprise that the median listing for a top-tier home is sixty-eight words long, while the median listing for a bottom-tier home is twenty words shorter, at only forty-seven words. A medium-tier home falls right in the middle, with its median listing employing sixty words to describe the home for sale. In all of these cases, however, the fundamental rule still applies: More words are better.

Again, of course, there's a caveat to this. At a certain point—around 250 words, to be exact—additional words won't help the final sale price. Those extra words won't hurt your final price, but it will waste your time and creativity to write a novel-length listing.

Instead of just adding extra words for the sake of it, you'd be much better off taking that time to choose the *right* words. If you're writing a listing description, don't waste words on vague euphemisms. Instead, you should stress your home's quality features like granite countertops and stainless-steel appliances. You should mention all the parts of your home that have recently been upgraded. You should make it clear that your home has concrete features that distinguish it from the place next door. Give buyers the information they want and need, because that's how you'll sell your home for more.

Remember, you've got up to 250 words to provide a detailed description of your home. And on this point, the numbers are clear: Describe your house in vivid detail—just don't write a Homeric poem about it.

FINDING "THE ONE"

In case it's not clear yet, the language of real estate listings is bogged down in secret rules and code words. It's a language where "modern" means the opposite, and "unique" is just about the worst thing you could be.

With so many words tethered to undesirable hidden meanings, it might seem almost impossible for a seller to break through the noise. It might seem equally impossible for a buyer to find the right house buried in endless misleading listings.

But we're confident that we've cracked the real estate code. And if you're mindful of the signals you're sending—and the signals you're getting—there's no reason you should wind up with a missed housing connection.

When Amy, our data-driven dater, set out on her research project, her goal was to see how women who got more dates presented themselves—and then to create a "super-profile" that combined the other women's successful tactics with her own personal information. In other words, she realized that it's not really about what the seller says. It's much more important to consider what the seller's words say to the buyer.

The same is true with real estate. And using data, we promise, your story can have a very happy ending. Just like Amy's.

Exterior of the Banks's family home from the 1991 movie *Father of the Bride* (*Photofest*)

March Madness

When to List Your Home

Across the country, home sales reach their peak in the month of June. In the last week of June alone, national residential real estate transactions are 40 percent higher than the average throughout the year. In colder climates, the peak comes a bit later in the summer. In warmer areas, a bit earlier in the spring. March, for instance, is the most popular time to buy and sell in Miami. In Chicago, meanwhile, sales are strongest in June and then again in August.

When you think about it, this makes perfect sense. What Chicagoan wants to trek through the slush to open houses in the middle of January? And what Floridian wants to house-hunt when it's 99 degrees and 99 percent humidity in August? If you take into account the weather—along with the inconvenience of families having to uproot their kids in the middle of the school year—it's no wonder that from coast to coast and border to border, the late spring and early summer are the most popular times to buy, sell, and move.

This climate-driven trend has clear implications for those thinking about putting their property on the market. There's no shortage of advice online about the best time to list, and it all goes something like this: The majority of home sales occur when the weather heats up, and homes sold during this time of year tend to attract high prices. Therefore, conventional wisdom tells us, it's best to list early in the year. That way, you're sure to benefit from the June peak in sales, and the premium pricing during the summer months as well. List too late, we're warned, and you could miss this warm weather bump.

At first blush, this conventional wisdom seems particularly wise. After all, there's one thing that all homeowners looking to sell have in common—they want to do so as *quickly* as possible, and for as much *money* as possible. Listing early, in theory, means more buyers looking to buy, and therefore a better chance of closing faster and for a good price.

But when you stop and think about it, this advice is rather imprecise—almost unhelpfully so. "Early in the year" could mean January 1, or April 30, or any date in between. Sure, it's good to know that September and November aren't the best months to list your home. But "early in the year"—a several month window— doesn't exactly narrow things down for sellers trying to navigate the complicated and high-stakes real estate market.

It turns out there's a good reason why the conventional wisdom about when to list is so vague. Until recently, there was simply no way to crunch the numbers to determine the most advantageous moment for homeowners to put their property on the market. This isn't because economists hadn't figured out the right method of *analysis*. Rather, economists hadn't had access to all the relevant *data*.

It all comes down to supply and demand. In order to identify the window when sellers have the best shot at selling quickly for the most money, you need good data on four important questions:

- When are buyers looking to buy?
- When are sellers looking to sell?
- When are these listings and sales taking place?
- Did the sale under-perform or over-perform?

For the first time, the answers to all these questions exist in the same place, readily available to consumers. And as a result, we can analyze the data to finally answer that simple question on every home seller's mind, the one that no one has been able to precisely answer until now:

When *exactly* should I list?

We have a unique perspective on the demand for residential real estate. Analyzing our Web traffic over the course of two years tells us an awful lot about when folks are looking to buy. For instance, we see a sharp spike in visitors making contact with real estate agents through Zillow's website and apps in the early spring, ramping up in the third week of April, and continuing into July. Contacting an agent is a clear indication that a prospective home buyer is getting serious about house-hunting. And sure enough, we can see that spike in agent *inquiries* translate into actual home *sales*. After the April spike in agent contacts, sales reach their highest levels nationwide just nine weeks later, at the end of June.

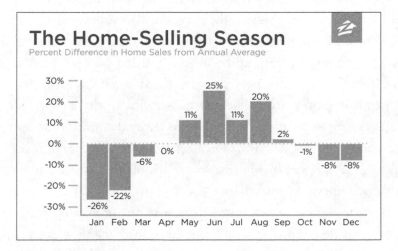

What does this all mean for prospective sellers? Well, if agent contacts crescendo in May and July, and home sales peak in the month of June (with a smaller bump in August), the conventional wisdom that sellers should list early in the year sure seems spot-on.

But, again, what does "early" mean? Is there such a thing as *too* early? Is there a sweet spot for listing your home so that it has the best chance of meeting your twin goals—that is, selling fast *and* for more money? And is there a measurable impact if you list before or after the peak?

The answer to all of these questions is a resounding *yes*. Our analysis shows that listing too early or too late *does* result in more time on the market and a lower sale price. There *is* a sweet spot when sellers should list, and hitting it can pay off to the tune of *thousands of dollars*.

To understand this goldilocks dynamic, let's now look at the supply side of the equation. After all, if there's weak demand, but a lot of supply, your home could languish on the market for months and then sell for less than it's worth. On the other hand, if there's strong demand and limited supply, that could trigger a bidding war for your property, which could mean a fast sale for a high price—exactly what every seller dreams of.

Here's what we can tell from analyzing four million homes that were listed on Zillow—in other words, the supply of homes for sale. Most sellers, perhaps unsurprisingly, follow the conventional wisdom. There is a large spike in newly listed homes "early in the year," and specifically between the third week in February and the beginning of March. The sellers who list in the late winter are clearly trying to position themselves to take advantage of the strong spring and summer demand. Then again, with all these new listings popping up at once, there are a lot of options for buyers, as well as a lot of competition for sellers.

But the data gives us more than just an interesting picture of supply and demand. It also tells us how long it takes every single listing to sell, how the sale price of each listing compares to the estimated home value at the time it was listed, and what kind of homes are on the market at any given time. That means we can pinpoint not just the season, but also the *exact weeks* when it's most opportune for sellers to list their homes.

Our analysis of the data shows that homes listed in the last weeks of March sold the fastest and for the most money. Interestingly, these "magic weeks" came *before* the peak in agent contacts (May and June), but just *after* the peak in newly listed homes (late February and early March). These listings tended to be slightly larger and more expensive homes, on average. But that's not why they performed better. Our analysis showed that these high-performing late-March listings didn't get lost in the sea of other new listings. *Just the opposite.*

Sure, there were more listings for buyers to look through after the peak in new listings, but the very *newest* listings—those posted after the peak, at the end of March—appeared at the *top* of the search results for prospective buyers who sort by listing date. Many buyers have already sifted through the available listings several times before they start getting serious about buying. By that point, those older listings will start looking stale, while these relatively new listings stand out from the pack and receive more attention, more offers, and more money as a result.

We're guessing that last part piqued your interest. And it should.

You've heard the old saying, "time is money." According to the data, *timing* is money, too. In 2011 and 2012, for instance, sellers who listed at the end of March didn't just sell *faster* than average. They sold for over 2 percent *more* than the average listing. Nationally, that translated into a premium worth more than four thousand dollars over the estimated value!

Of course, you don't sell your home nationally; you sell in your local market, and your competition is other homes in the immediate vicinity. This is an important consideration because, in some metro areas, the difference in sale price between listing during the peak and hitting the sweet spot just afterward can be significant.

Looking at sales in Seattle, for instance, homes listed in the window of opportunity sold for 2.8 percent higher than average, a premium of just under $6,500. Our analysis of sales in the Bay Area showed that listings during this time frame translated into a 5.9 percent premium for sellers, which netted them an average of $22,000 more than if they had listed during another period of the year!

There is another important regional factor to consider here—the weather. As we mentioned at the beginning of this chapter, home sales in warmer climates peak in the late spring, and colder climates peak in the early summer. The same goes for supply and demand. Peak listings shift earlier or later depending on the climate, as do agent contacts.

In Atlanta, for instance, the best week to list in 2011 was the third week in March. That same year in Boston, however, sellers had the best outcomes when they listed in the second week of April.

Despite these regional, largely weather-driven variations, wherever you live, if you're selling your home, *make sure you list after the first major influx of new listings for the year.*

Put your home on the market after you fill out your NCAA March Madness basketball brackets, but before someone slips on an ivy-green jacket at the Masters Golf Tournament at Augusta National.

Timing is money—and if you list at the wrong time, it can really cost you. In particular, homes listed in December tend to sell for much less than they otherwise would be expected to. Homes listed in Atlanta during the last week of December sold for 7 percent less than average. In Chicago, homes listed in the third week of December sold for a whopping 8.6 percent less. The holiday season might be the most wonderful time of the year for a lot of things, but selling a home just isn't one of them.

Maybe you're thinking that all this sounds impossible. Perhaps you're dubious about these "magic weeks" when listing your home can help you sell fast for top dollar. Well, there *is* a caveat here. These favorable windows aren't set in stone. They can and will shift each year, according to when new listings and agent contacts peak. And those factors, as we've discussed, can fluctuate depending on weather patterns. For instance, think about how an unusually

The Worst Week to List

Atlanta — December — ↓ -7.0%

Boston — December — ↓ -4.5%

Chicago — December — ↓ -8.6%

Dallas–Fort Worth — September — ↓ -3.0%

Miami–Fort Lauderdale — December — ↓ -4.3%

New York — December — ↓ -2.8%

San Francisco — December — ↓ -3.7%

Seattle — December — ↓ -6.9%

United States — December — ↓ -2.1%

= Percent Difference in Sale Price from Annual Average

warm winter in an especially cold city might shift the window of opportunity forward by a week or two from the year before.

While you can't *predict* these moments of opportunity, you can *detect* them. At the beginning of the home sales season, keep your eye on new listings in the neighborhood where you're selling your home. Monitor them as they ramp up and, most importantly, take note when they begin to slow down. That's when you know the time has come to put your home on the market.

It's kind of like making microwave popcorn. You don't want to stop the microwave too soon, because then you'll have a bunch of un-popped kernels sitting in the bottom of the bag. And you don't want to leave the bag in the microwave for too long, because all that delicious popcorn will start to burn. You have to listen to the pops to get the timing just right. When the rapid-fire popping trails off, *that's* when you grab the bag out of the microwave. And when the burst of new listings in the later winter or early spring trails off, *that's* when you should list your home.

Beverly House has been filmed for many movies, including *The Godfather* *(Photofest)*

Real Est8 4 Sale

Use Superstitions to Your Advantage

You may have noticed that this book has no Chapter 13, just as many buildings in the United States and other Western countries have no thirteenth floor. The reason: *superstitions*.

When it comes to our everyday lives, superstitions may be irrational, but they're not irrelevant. Due to the prevalence and power of superstitions across cultures, we wanted to determine what effect—if any—these lucky and unlucky numbers have on real estate transactions. Are buyers willing to pay a premium to avoid a hexed house? Or, conversely, will they dish out more cash for a lucky lodging?

The answer to both questions is, statistically speaking, yes.

ADDRESS FOR SUCCESS

But first, let's talk about paraskevidekatriaphobia.

No, we didn't just mash the keyboard in frustration. "Paraskevidekatriaphobia" is actually the technical—and tongue-twisting—term for anyone with a fear of Friday the Thirteenth.

Before you scoff, consider that an estimated 17 to 21 million Americans suffer from this phobia. Some are so terrified that Friday the Thirteenth will invite tragedy that they refuse to leave their houses. As a result, according to the Stress Management Center and Phobia Institute of North Carolina, the American economy loses a whopping *$800 to $900 million* from reduced activity every Friday the Thirteenth.[1] It's quite an inauspicious day, indeed.

Of course, "13" isn't the only number imbued with mystical powers. On the bad luck side, we also have "666," or as the book of Revelations calls it, "the number of the beast." (Fear of this satanic number is an even more unpronounceable "hexakosioihexekonta-hexaphobia.") And on the side of good fortune, we have the traditional "lucky 7," which is a favorite in Las Vegas. And we have another Biblical reference, "316," as in John 3:16—"For God so loved the world that he gave his one and only Son, that whoever believes in him shall not perish but have eternal life"—which you can find on everything from bumper stickers and billboards to the eye black of professional football players.

How do these numbers affect home sales?

It turns out that homes with "666" somewhere in the list price sell for 3.2 percent less than expected. Interestingly, however, we found that houses with "13" as the house number actually sell 2 percent *higher* than expected. (Note that there are less than half as many houses with "13" as the house number as with "12" or "14," probably for the same reason that older buildings are usually "missing" the thirteenth floor.)

Another surprising finding is that although "7" has long been viewed as a lucky number across cultures, it has a decidedly *unlucky* effect on sale price. At a slot machine on the Vegas strip, landing "777" means you hit the jackpot. But homes where "777" is the entire house number sell for a full 2.1 percent *less* than their estimated home value; house numbers that just include "777" (17779 Main St, for instance) sell for 1.8 percent *less* than theirs.

On the other hand, houses where the house number is only "7" do sell for 1.8 percent more than their estimated sale price. Having "316" in the house number also boosts the price of the home 1.2 percent more than expected.

In other words, finding the right home outweighs superstition across cultures—at least when it comes to house numbers.

While superstitious sellers would find it difficult—or, more realistically, impossible—to alter their address to include a lucky number or omit an unlucky one, changing the sale price of a house is a piece of cake. In theory, then, list prices might reflect any superstitious tendencies in American real estate.

Indeed, that's precisely what we found in analyzing 4.5 million homes listed for sale on Zillow.

KNOW THE SUPERSTITIONS OF YOUR LOCAL MARKET

In order to figure out whether superstitions are statistically significant in list prices, we put away our Ouija board and used the data to examine the influence of the highly superstitious numbers "4" and "8."

In Chinese culture, the number "8"—pronounced *"ba"* in Mandarin—sounds very similar to the word for "prosper" or "wealth," and is considered very lucky. The two digits "88" also look like the character for "double joy." "4," by contrast, sounds nearly identical to the word for "death."

The way these divergent digits play out in Asian society is striking. For the same reason that Western buildings omit the thirteenth level, you won't see many Asian skyscrapers with a fourth floor. In Hong Kong, many buildings don't just leave out the fourth floor, but any floor that has a "4" in its number (e.g., the 4th, 14th, 24th, 34th, and 40th through 49th). That means you can come across a fifty-story building that only has thirty-six floors! And because "8" is believed to influence financial luck, items with "8" in them are considered highly valuable—so much so that a man in Chengdu, China, sold a telephone number composed entirely of "8"s for $270,723. And it's no coincidence that the beautifully choreographed opening ceremony of the 2008 Beijing Summer Olympic Games began precisely at 8:08 p.m. on 8/8/08.

To quantify the influence of "4" and "8" on real estate transactions, we evaluated list prices where the *last non-zero digit* in the list price was either a "4" or an "8" to determine whether the house had a lucky or unlucky price. For instance, we looked at cases where the list price was $180,000 or $274,000, while also allowing for non-round list prices such as $300,008 or $400,040. So, when we say that a list price "ended" in a "4" or an "8," what we're really talking about is the last non-zero digit in the list price.*

In order to gauge the effect of "lucky 8" and "unlucky 4" on American real estate, we compared the incidence of list prices ending in a "4" or an "8" along with the percentage of the population that is of Chinese descent in a given ZIP code. If imparting luck into the sale of your house by including lucky numbers in the list price is important to sellers of Chinese descent, then in heavily Chinese areas we would expect to see more houses with list prices that end in an "8" and fewer list prices that end in a "4."

Notice anything? As we predicted, the "8 rate" in all of the listed areas is well above the national average. We also see that the

Lucky and Unlucky List Prices

ZIP Code	City	Percent of Chinese Residents	Percent of Listings Ending in 4	Percent of Listings Ending in 8
	United States	1.2%	2.5%	3.8%
91801	Alhambra, CA	38.5%	1.9%	25.7%
91007	Arcadia, CA	40.9%	0.3%	50.2%
91755	Monterey Park, CA	52.3%	1.3%	31.3%
91754	Monterey Park, CA	39.7%	0.5%	30.2%
11355	New York, NY	45.8%	0.7%	27.3%
94133	San Francisco, CA	44.2%	0.0%	6.1%
94134	San Francisco, CA	39.7%	0.5%	13.8%
94116	San Francisco, CA	37.7%	0.5%	14.9%
91776	San Gabriel, CA	41.4%	1.7%	33.3%
91780	Temple City, CA	39.2%	1.3%	42.3%

Source: U.S. Census Bureau and Zillow

---

* A quick word on methodology: We focused on the last digit because even the most superstitious seller would be unlikely to price their $450,000 house at $399,000— setting themselves up for a $51,000 loss—just to avoid the number "4" in the list price. But they could pretty easily price their house at $458,000 rather than at $450,000. Changing the last non-zero digit of the price only slightly alters the listing price, and in doing so, sellers can satiate their superstitions without risking their potential profits.

areas with high Chinese populations have far fewer list prices that end in "4"s than the national average. The greater the Chinese population in a particular ZIP code, the more listings that end in lucky numbers, and the fewer listings that end in unlucky numbers. But what we really want to know is: Does having a lucky or unlucky number in your list price actually affect your sale price?

To answer that question, we analyzed the sale-to-estimated-home-value ratio of homes with the list price ending in 4 or 8, in ZIP codes where the Chinese population density is more than 10 percent. For homes in areas where less than 10 percent of the population is of Chinese descent, having an "8" as the last non-zero digit results in *a negligible difference in price*. However, in areas where *more* than 10 percent of the population is of Chinese descent, homes with a listing price ending in "8" sell for *1.5 percent more* than the home's value. That works out to an additional $2,400 on the median US house.

So in heavily Chinese areas, the number "8" not only *sounds* like "wealth"—it actually leads to it! "Eight" is, indeed, great.

On the other hand, homes that have a listing price that ends in "4" sell for less than expected. In non-Chinese areas, we see that homes with a "4" as the last non-zero digit in the list price sell for 0.4 percent less than homes whose list prices end in other numbers—a small, albeit statistically significant, reduction.

However, for homes in areas where the Chinese population is greater than 10 percent, the effect is far greater—and more negative. In places with large Chinese populations, having a "4" in the listing price lowers the sale a full 1 percent below the estimated sale price.

So, if you happen to be selling your home in an area with lots of people of Chinese descent, it's well worth being aware of numeric cultural significance when pricing your home. Listing at $158,000 instead of $154,000 may help to attract a buyer and add a little luck into your real estate adventures. At the very least, according to Zillow's database, it's a lot more effective than crossing your fingers and knocking on wood.

Exterior of the McCallister family home from the movie *Home Alone* (*Photofest*)

15

The Price Is Right

How to Determine Your Asking Price

If you've ever spent a sick day at home channel surfing, you've probably come across an episode of the long-running game show and staple of daytime television, *The Price Is Right*. For more than forty years, contestants on *The Price Is Right* have attempted to win prizes by guessing the retail price of featured products, from cars to cans of cream of mushroom soup. Contestants who guess closest to—but not above—the actual retail price of an item get to claim it as their prize. Guess too high, however, and all you get is a pat on the back from the host, Drew Carey (or, before he retired, Bob Barker), as one of his assistants escorts you off-stage.

Pricing your house for sale is a lot like playing *The Price Is Right*. If you want to take home a prize—i.e., a quick sale for a great price—you should list your home for as close as possible to, but not above, its market value. Just like on the game show, there is a real danger to overpricing.

Understandably, most sellers are more afraid of *underpricing* than overpricing. After all, no one wants to sell his or her home for less than it's worth. Indeed, that's why some sellers purposely overprice. They assume that by listing high, they'll somehow drive up the sale price and net some extra cash. But in reality, this strategy rarely works. In fact, it almost always backfires. The very tactic that sellers hope will inflate the final sale price ends up lowering it instead. So why do we do it?

Consider two imaginary families: the Barkers and the Careys. They live in the same neighborhood and own identical houses that were built the very same year. Both homes have three bedrooms and two bathrooms. Both have a Jacuzzi in the master bath, a fancy fireplace in the family room, and granite countertops in the kitchen.

The estimated value for these homes is, not surprisingly, the same: $200,000.

The Barkers are avid watchers of *The Price Is Right*, so they understand the importance of, well, getting the price right. They list their home for $200,000—even though they purchased it for $225,000 in 2006—and the market rewards them. Their open house is flooded with potential buyers, several of whom make offers and start a small bidding war. After only a few weeks on the market, the Barkers have signed a contract for $204,000. They not only sold quickly, but they sold for more—$4,000 more than their asking price.

The Careys, however, are a different story. They're convinced that their home is worth far more than $200,000. After all, they paid $210,000 when they bought it in 2009! And so the Careys put their house on the market for $220,000—10 percent more than the Barkers' identical house.

You can probably guess what happens: The Careys' house doesn't sell. After four open houses without any visitors—much less any offers—the Careys knock the price down to $210,000, a 4.5 percent price cut. But that's still not nearly enough; at $210,000, the house is still priced 5 percent over its market value.

Weeks turn into months with still no offer, and the Careys grow increasingly discouraged as they continue to pay an expensive mortgage on a house they no longer want. Finally, they take a deep breath and cut the price yet again, this time by more than 5 percent, to $200,000. Unfortunately, it's too little, too late. Even though the new price does reflect their home's estimated market value, the listing has already lingered for months, and potential buyers know it. In the past, only real estate agents and professionals knew how long homes sat on the market. But now there are online resources where people can easily identify stale listings like the Careys' house. Now, when potential buyers see a stale listing like this, they start to wonder what's wrong. They start to expect a lower price.

The Careys may have priced high for fear of leaving money on the table, but sadly, their overpricing strategy results in the outcome they feared the most. They eventually find a buyer who offers $188,000, which is $16,000 and 6 percent less than the Barkers made on their identical home. But the Careys have no choice, and they accept far less than they had hoped for.

According to our data, sellers fall into "The Price Is Wrong" trap more often than you might think. When it comes to setting the list price of homes, roughly half of sellers are like the Barkers, and the rest are, to varying degrees, like the Careys.

We tracked more than a million homes listed for sale and found that 47 percent end up cutting their list price in order to sell. On average, sellers overprice their homes by about 6.9 percent. However, a small percentage of homes are so dramatically overpriced that sellers have to reduce the price by as much as 15 percent in order to attract a buyer.

The majority of homes with price cuts—57.4 percent—only need one reduction in order to sell. Most sellers see their home languishing on the market, recognize their mistake, correct the list price, and find a buyer sooner rather than later. But some sellers are stubborn and don't cut enough the first time, which necessitates further price cuts down the road. A quarter of overpriced homes need a second price cut, and some homes need several. A small fraction of overpriced homes, just over 1 percent, need six or more price cuts in order to sell.

The data tells us that when a listing is overpriced, it tends to sell for *less* than its estimated market value. In fact, the more a home is overpriced, and the larger the price cut it needs to sell, the bigger the impact on the final sale price.

For example, a house that undergoes a price cut of 10 percent has, on average, a sale price that is nearly 2 percent less than its estimated value. That's a 4 percent spread between homes that are priced correctly and those that are overpriced. While this may not sound like a lot, it adds up fast. A seller who overprices a $400,000 home by 10 percent is making a mistake that could potentially cost $16,000!

Of course, overpricing your house doesn't only cost you money; it also costs you time. Here, again, the bigger a seller's mistake in pricing, the bigger the impact on the sale. In our sample, homes that were correctly priced and needed no price cut spent an average of 107 days on the market as of the beginning of 2013—although this number changes over time depending on market conditions. Listings that need, for example, a 10 percent price cut spend an average of 220 days on the market. That's more than twice as long and a difference of almost four months. Naturally, the more you overprice your house to begin with, the longer your house spends on the market, and the lower the sale price will be.

Just like on our favorite game show, however, there's a big reward for those who resist the urge to overprice. When contestants on *The Price Is Right* guess the exact retail price of an item, they receive a bonus prize. And in real estate, sellers who price their house at the real, fair market value tend not only to sell faster, but also to sell for 2 percent *more* than their home is worth.

Price cuts are dispiriting for sellers. Having to trim your list price in order to attract potential buyers compounds the highly stressful experience of selling a home with further anxiety and disappointment. But the best thing to do when you've overpriced your home is to take your lumps and cut the price all the way to its true market value.

PANTS ON FIRE

When public figures are caught fibbing, savvy PR professionals advise that they come clean as soon as possible. Admitting a lie isn't easy, but it's better in the end. Otherwise, the cover-up may be worse than the crime.

The same goes with pricing your home for sale. If you overprice, it's better to admit your mistake and cut the price *all the way down* to the true market value in one fell swoop. The alternative is "death by a thousand cuts"—price cut after price cut—which only serves to drag out the ordeal and compound the problem. Your home lingers on the market, real estate agents describe the listing with the dreaded adjective "stale," and buyers smell blood in the water.

That's what happened to the Careys. And it's what happened to a lot of sellers in the wake of the housing bubble.

The extent to which sellers overprice their homes depends, in part, on *when* they purchased it and for how much. Sellers who bought in January 2006 overprice their homes by only 8 percent, while those who bought in January 2009 overprice by 22 percent. In other words, homeowners who purchased in the run-up to the housing bubble seem to be more willing to confront current market realities, whereas sellers who purchased their homes during or after 2009 have trouble coming to terms with the extent to which their investment has been devalued.

As a result, sellers who bought their homes during or after 2009 generally price their homes 10 percent higher than the amount for which they purchased it only one to two years ago. In other words, they're listing their homes as though they have *appreciated* in value since 2009, when, in fact, the national real estate market *depreciated* 10 percent since 2009. That means many of these sellers are overpricing their homes by a significant amount: roughly 20 percent above market value.

And as we've discussed, that never ends well.

Suddenly, the Careys' predicament makes a bit more sense. While the Barkers purchased their home in 2006, before the housing market tanked, the Careys purchased in 2009, after the bubble had burst. The Careys priced their home 25 percent above its actual value because they assumed—wrongly—that they had escaped the worst of the housing crash. In reality, the bubble didn't pop all at once; it slowly deflated over four and a half years. When the Careys purchased their home for $225,000 in 2009, it was still overvalued. By 2012, their home was only worth $200,000. Not wanting to face facts, they mistakenly, and significantly, overpriced their home.

The data clearly shows that it's hard for some homeowners to come to grips with their property's diminished value, especially when faced with the prospect of selling for a loss. But the data also clearly shows that the best course of action for sellers is to price their homes as close to fair market value as possible, in order to avoid price cuts that end up slicing into their profits. That's the best way to ensure that the price will always be right.

The Ricardos in the living room of their home in the TV show *I Love Lucy* (CBS/ *Photofest*)

16

Nine Is the Magic Number

How to Sell for More by Asking for Less

During the early 1980s, Dave Gold discovered his destiny in a Los Angeles liquor store.

As Dave told the *Los Angeles Times*, he was running the shop with his wife when they started to notice a strange pattern: They would charge $0.98 or $1.02 for a bottle of wine, and it would sell fine, without ever selling out. When Dave set the sale price at ninety-nine cents, however, the wine would jump off the shelves in no time at all.[1]

There was just something about that ninety-nine-cent price. Or, as Dave put it, "I realized it was a magic number."[2]

In 1982, Dave opened America's first 99¢ Only Store in Los Angeles. His store sold practically everything—kitchen gadgets, dog food, hair products, you name it—all for ninety-nine cents. It was as if he had built a rocket ship to riches. Dave was a multimillionaire by the time he died in 2013. The store he founded became a chain that boasted almost three hundred locations across the United States.

Dave Gold may have made a fortune from his magic number, but he was hardly the only person to discover the power of prices ending in "9." Psychological pricing, as this practice is called, pops up everywhere from candy aisles to high-end fashion boutiques. And for good reason: It works.

In one study, researchers looked at a women's clothing retailer and found that products sold 8 percent more when they were priced to end in ".99" instead of ".00."[3]

In another experiment, researchers marketed the exact same item for thirty-four dollars, thirty-nine dollars, and forty-four dollars. The thirty-four-dollar and forty-four-dollar products sold in about the same quantity. But the thirty-nine-dollar product out-performed both.[4]

Is the number "9" really imbued with mystical powers? Or is something else going on?

It's a question that has sparked endless debate among retailers, advertisers, and psychologists. Do our minds automatically round prices down, so we perceive a penny saved as much more than that? Does a price that ends in "9" signify "discount" in our minds, drawing us to a product whether or not it's really on sale? Do we just like the shape of the number "9"?

Nothing explains this phenomenon completely. But whatever the hypothesis, one fact is clear: The number "9" *can* perform a magic trick. It allows a seller to lower his or her prices, and still make more money.

And after crunching the numbers, we can affirm: This is just as true in real estate as it is in other industries.

On average, a home will sell for more—and often, sell faster—if its original price ends in a "9" instead of a "0." *You really can make more by asking for less.*

To be clear, when we're looking at homes that cost hundreds of thousands of dollars, we're not talking about ending the price in "ninety-nine cents." Indeed, you don't see many homes listed for $150,000.99

Instead, the psychological power in a home price resides in the last digit that isn't a zero. So, for instance, $149,000 and $149,900 are both examples of strategic home prices.

And when you think about it, on some basic level, don't those prices just *feel* more appealing?

Now, imagine two houses. They're identical in every way—same size, same number of bathrooms, and so on. They even have the same estimated home value of $150,000. The only difference is that, for some reason, one homeowner decided to put her house on the market for $149,000, and the other seller priced his home at $150,000. *Remarkably, our data shows that the house that initially is priced for less will ultimately sell for an average of $2,175 more, just because of that magic number "9."* What's more, when we mined the data, we found that this dynamic works at many different price points, for all kinds of homes.

First we looked at homes with a "9" in the thousands place. In other words, we compared homes priced at $110,000 to homes priced at $109,000—homes priced at $850,000 were compared to homes priced at $849,000—and so on.

After they were sold, we compared each home's final price to its estimated value. In almost every case, the home with the "9" sold for slightly more than the home with the "0." When we compiled these differences, we saw that sellers could exploit a clear advantage by ending their home prices with the number "9" in the last non-zero digit.

Of course, home sellers obviously *do* need to decrease their asking prices to see this final sale price gain. It's worth it, however, because the amount gained by using psychological pricing is greater than the discount. In other words, the risk a seller takes by cutting a thousand dollars from their asking price is usually rewarded with more than a thousand dollars added on to the final price. In fact, the reward is usually much greater than that, as the bar chart on the next page makes clear.

The percent effect of the number "9" on sale price does begin to diminish as homes become more expensive. This makes sense intuitively, since, as a home's price climbs, its buyer is less likely to consider the marginal difference of those last thousand dollars.

That said, it also becomes less costly for the seller to offer this discount as the price goes higher. Taking $1,000 off the price of a

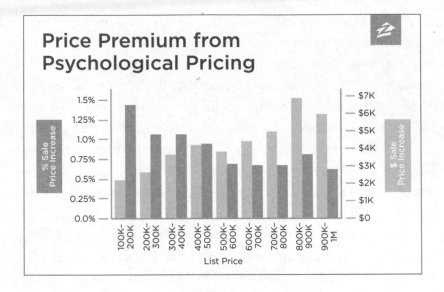

$100,000 home is a 1 percent discount. But shaving $1,000 off of a $1,000,000 price is only a 0.1 percent discount. So there's not much potential downside if a seller takes the risk with a strategic price. In addition, while the supernatural power of "9" may fade as the price climbs higher, its impact never totally disappears. Even at much higher price points, the number "9" still seems to exert a psychological pull that can't be ignored. And that's not all. A home priced at $449,000 does not just sell for more than a home priced at $450,000; it sells quicker, too.

Across our dataset, we found that homes using psychological pricing in the thousands digit sold anywhere from four days to a full week faster. Overall, comparing all homes with psychological pricing to their counterparts priced at $1,000 more, the homes with psychological pricing sold 4.2 days (3 percent) faster on average than the homes without psychological pricing.

Putting a "9" at the end even has power to work some magic for sellers when the price is only $100 less—when, say, a seller lists his or her home for $100,900 instead of $101,000. Just by shaving a hundred dollars off of your initial ask—a piddling 0.09 percent of the total price—you can ultimately sell your house for over a thousand dollars more!

The number "9"'s power once again diminishes as homes become more expensive. However, just as in the previous example, the effect of the number "9" never fully goes away. Which brings us back to our original question: Why? What causes this phenomenon?

The best answer may lie in the very early stages of the house-hunting process. In these initial moments of excitement and anxiety, buyers tend to look at an unending stream of listings, photographs, and numbers. They're drinking from a fire hose, not a water glass.

Given the massive volume of data that buyers must scrutinize—and the enormous emotion and pressure associated with a major, life-altering financial transaction—one home's smallest comparative advantage may be just enough to give a buyer pause, and to make them linger a moment longer than they otherwise might. In other words, a price that ends in "9" may be just the thing that cuts through the clutter.

That's especially true when you consider how people search for home listings online. Most people who look for homes online sort their results by price. So let's say that you plan to put your home on the market for $150,000. If you price it at $149,900 instead, your listing will show up higher in their search results when sorted from low price to high. That tiny advantage alone could distinguish your listing from all the other homes that are listed for $150,000. Strategically pricing your home like this is a small way to get your home noticed, but sometimes that's enough. An initial attraction like this can lead someone to fall in love with a home. And as we all know, when you're in love, you'll go to great lengths to win the object of your desire. You might bid higher or push to close the sale faster—especially if other people have also felt the same love-at-first-sight spark.

Maybe Dave Gold was right. When you're selling your home, "9" might be a magic number after all.

Exterior of Dunphy family home from the TV show *Modern Family (Photofest)*

Appraising Real Estate Agents

Reviews Correlate with Performance

Once you start looking for them, they're hard to miss. The signs pop up in front yards and on park benches, on billboards and bulletin boards. In Battle Creek, Michigan: "Everything we touch turns to SOLD!"[1] In Jamison, Pennsylvania: "Scott Geller, the Home Seller."[2] In Hutchinson, Kansas: "The Spouses who Sell Houses."[3]

These are *real* real estate ads. And they're everywhere.

Based on their publicity, these real estate professionals seem too good to be true. But of course, we know that real estate agents aren't all superheroes. No matter how appealing their ads may be, some of them can take months and months to sell your home. They may advise you to jump at the first offer, no matter how low, or they may recommend that you wait for a "right" offer that might never come. On the other hand, the best real estate agents can offer great advice on how to sell your home faster. They can be invaluable allies if you want to get a higher price for your home (and who doesn't want that?).

When it comes to real estate agents, we're all looking for the same thing: We want an agent with local knowledge that rivals a longtime neighbor, and the negotiating skills to match the secretary of state.

But how do you find that person? Because, clearly, it's not enough to go by the advertisements. And you sure can't just pick a name out of the phone book (because you probably don't have one).

If you're searching for a real estate agent, you can always ask friends and neighbors for a recommendation. You can read online reviews. You can even ask for references. But after analyzing more than one million sales by agents in our database, we have a few other tips for cutting through the slogans and the smiling head-shots. We can tell you how to appraise real estate agents—and how to tell when you've found the best one in town.

WHY REAL ESTATE AGENTS ARE MORE IMPORTANT THAN EVER

Before we get to that, though, we realize this might sound need-lessly complicated to you. Maybe you're wondering whether we still need real estate agents at all. You might be wondering if they're heading the way of the travel agent, the stockbroker, and, well, the dodo bird.

We get this question all the time. And our answer is simple: No. Not by a long shot.

Real estate agents are still incredibly important, and they're not going anywhere. In fact, real estate professionals are working more than ever today. According to a recent survey, almost 90 percent of home buyers used an agent to help buy their home. In 2001, that number was only 70 percent.[4]

In part, real estate agents have stayed relevant because they have embraced technology more than almost any other service-based industry. Almost every real estate professional has a website, and most of them have had these sites for years. They get in touch using text messages, use smart phones, and are active on social media.

But that's not the only reason that real estate agents are still thriving. They're more important than ever in part because we've all seen how complicated the housing market can be. We've seen how consequential these decisions are—and how devastating it is when home buying goes wrong. Given how life altering a home purchase can be, it's not really a surprise that more people than ever want a trained professional in their corner during the process.

This isn't just an anecdotal assumption. There's actually an entire field of economics called "transaction cost economics" that helps us understand why real estate professionals are likely to remain a part of the transactional process. (Please give us a moment to adjust our propeller hats.)

Among other things, transaction cost economics asks why professions such as real estate agents, stockbrokers, or travel agents exist in the first place. In theory, the market would be much more efficient without these "intermediating" firms in the middle. But as transaction cost economics explains, when a purchase is relatively infrequent and expensive, people are more likely to want a professional minding and managing the transaction. The more frequent and the less expensive a purchase is, the less necessary a middleman becomes.

This is why travel agents and stockbrokers are becoming extinct, while real estate professionals are still prospering. After all, when booking a trip to Pittsburgh, we're comfortable clicking "purchase" on our own. When finding and financing a home, however, the emotionally charged, life-changing, bank-account-draining gravity of the situation leads us to crave—and, indeed, to require—an expert's guidance.

In our eyes, a helpful analogy here is WebMD, the large and popular online health resource. We've all searched online to research our ailments—"what are the symptoms of Strep Throat?"—but then we go to a doctor for a proper diagnosis. We need professionals to help us interpret and treat what anyone with an Internet connection can find in twelve seconds on Google. The doctor's role, then, is a little different, but it's definitely not diminished.

The same is true of the real estate agent. Home purchases are infrequent, emotional, and expensive. High stakes command high expertise. But that doesn't mean people shouldn't be armed with the best possible information to help them navigate the process.

That also doesn't mean the real estate industry won't ever change. In fact, the job of a real estate professional is already evolving. Agents have evolved from the days when a large part of their job was being an information gatekeeper; today, theirs is more of a service industry, where they bring their minds and muscles to negotiating and pricing. People may be more and more comfortable searching for a home on their own—but they still want, and need, an agent there to help broker the final transaction and bargain for a fair price.

If you're one of those people who still wants a real estate agent by your side, you're clearly not alone. But remember, it's important to find the *right* agent. For the rest of this chapter, we'll give you some tips to make sure that you do.

THE SUPER-SELLERS

Before we go any further, we should note that real estate agents tend to specialize. Some focus on helping you buy a home, while others focus on selling. In this chapter, we're going to focus on seller's agents, aka listing agents, because we want to answer the question asked by virtually every person who's ever sold a home: "How do I find the agent who can sell my home for the highest price in the least amount of time?" Of course, sellers also pay the agent commissions, as much as 6 percent of the sales price of the home—so the stakes for sellers are particularly high when it comes to finding the right real estate agent.

When looking for someone to sell your home, it makes intuitive sense to seek out a person with a proven track record. If a real estate professional moves a lot of homes every year, that's an indicator that they can sell *your* home, too.

Of course, not all real estate agents are created equal—in that regard or any other. Some sell a huge number of homes every year, and some sell only one or two. Indeed, it's a little known fact that there is a subset of "super-sellers" who sell many of the homes in the United States.

When people talk about wealth distribution in America, they invariably point out that a tiny number of people control almost all of the money. One percent of Americans hold 40 percent of the wealth in the United States.[5] It's the same with real estate agents who specialize in selling homes, though it's not quite as extreme. The top 1 percent of seller's agents sell 8.7 percent of the homes in the United States. The top 10 percent of seller's agents sell a commanding 41 percent of all the homes. (For the purposes of this calculation, we're counting all homes equally. In other words, these are percentages of the total number of homes sold every year, not the total dollar value of home sales every year.)

To put some concrete numbers on those percentages, this means the real estate 1-percenters each sell at least twenty-two homes every year. The 10-percenters sell an average of seven homes every year. Compare that to the median agent in our sample, who sells a respectable two homes every year. There's a clear divide between the top sellers and everyone else. It's like a mountain, and the super-sellers have scaled it to the top.

IS THE SUPER-SELLER THE ONE TO HIRE?

So, you might be thinking, how do I find one of these super-sellers? Well, you should start by looking for agents with experience. Experienced real estate agents sell the most homes every year, and they're much more likely to be among the top sellers of the real estate world.

When we compared agents with greater than ten years of experience with agents who have been on the job for fewer than five years, we found that the experienced agents sell *twice* as many homes. It was the same when we looked at agents who've been working for a period of between five and ten years. They sell one-and-a-half times more homes than the agents who are new to the job.

In other words, if an agent with fewer than five years of experience sells two homes each year, then an agent with five to ten years of experience is likely to sell three homes. An agent with more than ten years of experience is likely to sell four homes.

Nevertheless, there's an enormous caveat to all this. Even if an agent sells a lot of houses, that doesn't necessarily mean they're the right person to sell *your* house. Actually, if you want the best price and the fastest sale, you need to take several other factors into account.

For one, experience actually can be a doubled-edged sword for a real estate professional. Everyone wants the most experienced agent, so these agents almost always have the most clients. That means they have more homes to keep track of, more showings to schedule, and more people to stay in touch with. Fitting in all of these extra appointments can mean that every client gets a little less time and a little less attention. Unsurprisingly, all of this extra business can slow an agent down. Compared to the newbies with less than five years' experience, agents who have been at it for ten to thirty years usually take a week longer to sell a home. Agents with thirty or forty years' experience take *two* extra weeks as compared to the group of new agents.

To be clear, these experienced agents usually aren't sagely waiting for a better offer that's just over the horizon. Our data shows no statistical difference in final sale price between a home sold by a thirty-year veteran and a home sold by a three-year rookie, even when taking the extra time on the market into account.

When you're looking for someone to help sell your home, it makes instinctive sense to turn to the most experienced person you can find. They've been in this game a long time, and it might give you peace of mind to know that you're in experienced hands. They probably have a lot of connections, and they can most likely give you the kind of advice that no one else can. But if the thing you're looking for is a higher sale price, the data says it doesn't matter how long your agent has been on the job. Experience might bring wisdom, but it doesn't necessarily put more cash in your pocket.

WHO MAKES BETTER AGENTS: MEN OR WOMEN?

Of course, finding the best real estate agent is much more complicated than just looking at experience. Real estate professionals also bring countless other personal qualities into the transaction that can affect your final sale price—including, in the aggregate, gender. Does that mean you should take gender into account when you're choosing a real estate agent? Not necessarily. But just in case you're curious (we were) we ran the numbers. One of us (Stan) thought men would be better. The other (Spencer) thought women. So we bet a two-dollar bill.

Imagine two real estate agents: Jack and Jill. They're each contracted to be the listing agent for two identical homes with spacious bedrooms, granite countertops, and a giant backyard. The home's estimated values clock in at $300,000.

Based on our analysis, Jack and Jill are both going to sell this house without any problem. But they'll probably go about it in different ways, and they'll almost certainly wind up with slightly different results.

Jill takes a look at the house and feels pretty optimistic. Jill may not know how dangerous it can be to overprice a home, so she lists the house at $320,700. Over the next few weeks, Jill meets with prospective buyers, explains about the great local schools, and shows off the three-car garage. After three months on the market, Jill sells the house for $290,550.

In Jack's parallel universe, he doesn't overprice the home by as much. When he gets to the house, he sets his price a little lower, at

$318,300. He buys some online ads, hosts open houses, and after a little more than three months, Jack sells the house for $289,650.

So who was the better agent? That depends on your criteria.

Jill ultimately got a higher price for the house, but she also had to take a steeper discount from her original listing price. Jack had a slightly sharper instinct about where to set the list price. Although he ultimately sold for slightly less than Jill compared to the home's value, he didn't have to discount his initial listing price by as much, and the sale prices ended up less than a thousand dollars apart.

This is a trend we see across the real estate market. Overall, female agents tend to take larger discounts off of their list prices. When we compared final sale prices to original list prices, we found that male agents sell homes for an average of 0.4 percentage points closer to the original list price. For the hypothetical $300,000 home, that 0.4 percent adds up to $1,200.

In short, men are ruthless appraisers, but more stubborn on price. Women, on the other hand, are more optimistic on pricing, but also more likely to drop the price to close a deal.

However, this doesn't mean that men are the superior sellers. Far from it. Remember, Jill got the slightly higher price in the end. What's more, female agents tend to sell their homes faster. In this case, Jill sold the house two and a half days faster than Jack. On average, homes sold by women agents spend 2 percent less time on the market.

That extra speed can be valuable. Still, before you declare victory for the women, it's worth noting that Jack is probably selling more homes than Jill. That's because male agents sell an average of 4 percent more homes every year than female agents.

So what does all this mean?

The difference between the genders is incredibly small, but it *is* statistically significant. When we control for all attributes of a home, women sell for higher prices *and* sell faster. In our minds, that makes them the victors in this battle of the sexes.

Spencer wins!

WHEN IN DOUBT, READ THE REVIEWS

If you want to learn more about a prospective agent, you can always read the online reviews. But if you're like us, you've probably wondered how reliable those reviews really are. After all, most of these assessments don't include a full name. If you're putting decades of your life's savings into this agent's hands, you should feel confident that their ratings reflect useful information, and not just personal opinions.

That's why we decided to test our evaluations. Over the last few years, buyers and sellers have written more than 600,000 reviews of local real estate agents they've worked with on Zillow. On top of the written reviews, people also have the chance to grade their agent on "local knowledge," "process expertise," "responsiveness," and "negotiation skills." For every category, the agent receives a score from 1 to 5, with 5 being perfect.

We lined these grades up against real sales data for each agent, and it turns out these ratings are actually a pretty accurate way to predict how an agent will do.

For instance, agents with a perfect "Responsiveness" rating of 5 sell homes 27 percent faster, on average, than agents with a responsiveness rating of 1. This amounts to an average of 106 days on the market for the most responsive agents versus 145 days for less responsive agents in the sample. That's a five-and-a-half week difference.

The story is similar with "local knowledge" scores. Agents with a perfect local knowledge rating sell 57 percent more homes than agents who rate only a 1. On average, that means the most knowledgeable agents sell eleven homes each year, while less knowledgeable agents sell only seven.

Not surprisingly, agents who are actively involved with other agents and consumers also tend to be better agents. One way we can measure that involvement is to see how many times agents have participated in our online forums, answering questions from

ordinary people. And we've found that agents who have participated in those forums at least five times sell, on average, 33 percent
more homes than agents who haven't participated.

If agents are good networkers, that's a good sign, too. We keep
track of whether agents work with their clients to find loan offi-
cers, contractors, and other service people they need while buying a
home. Again, the more connected agents are much more successful.
Just by providing five of these kinds of endorsements, an agent is
likely to sell an average of 20 percent more homes every year.

It's no surprise that the agents who are willing to go the extra
mile tend to be the most successful. But you don't have to guess who
those agents are. With just a few clicks of the mouse, you can now
see who really cares, and who's going to give your sale the attention
it deserves. These are the factors that distinguish a great real estate
agent. And once you find one, you'll know that you've found the
right agent for you.

THE DATA-HOOD

A NEW LOOK AT OUR NATION OF NEIGHBORHOODS

Set of Will Truman's living room from the TV show *Will and Grace* (NBC/
Photofest)

The Gayborhood Phenomenon

Property Values as a Bellwether of Social Change

American history has always been real estate history, and in each generation social conditions and the concept of home have been inextricably entwined. Take the first wave of seventeenth- and eighteenth-century American immigrants, setting out over the horizon for a new world in which land was available and affordable—and where they could practice their religion without fear of persecution. Consider the millions of Irish and German newcomers between the 1820s and the 1870s—and the millions more Jewish and Italian immigrants between the 1880s and 1920s. Despite their different ethnicities and points of origin, they all came to America in pursuit of economic opportunity and homeownership, certainly. But they also came for the welcoming communities their fellow immigrants had established.

The same could be said of migration *within* North America— from countryside to city, and from farm to factory. For instance, more than six million African Americans fled the rural South for northern cities during the Great Migration in the twentieth century. They weren't only escaping *from* a toxic history of slavery, racism, and discrimination; they were leaving *for* vibrant new communities in burgeoning urban economies.

These patterns of exodus are the tectonic plates that have moved American history. And they haven't stopped shifting.

We'll admit it, we kind of geek out when today's real estate data gives us a window onto the ways that our society is *still* changing— right now, before our very eyes. In fact, it turns out that real estate data tells an especially interesting and important story about the expansion of rights for the lesbian, gay, bisexual, and transgender (LGBT) community during the past several decades—and now well into the twenty-first century.

Many of us have sensed, for years, that LGBT communities throughout the country have driven gentrification and increased local property values. Recently, scholars have made an interesting empirical case to support this anecdotal hunch.

For instance, David Christafore of Konkuk University in Seoul, Korea, and Susane Leguizamon of Tulane University in New Orleans looked at home values in and around Columbus, Ohio, during the early 2000s. Specifically, they compared neighborhoods that supported gay marriage and neighborhoods that opposed it. What they found is that in pro-marriage-equality neighborhoods, every additional gay couple (in a neighborhood of 1,000 house-holds) raised property values by 1.1 percent. In anti-gay-marriage neighborhoods, every additional gay couple contributed to a decline in property values by 1 percent.

In other words, the real estate data directly reflects the varying social conditions, both positive and negative, for LGBT communi-ties in different parts of the country. It's a fascinating—and, yes, disturbing—window into the LGBT community's ongoing fight for acceptance and equality.[1]

It turns out, a broader look at historical housing data sheds further light on the trajectory of the LGBT rights movement. In fact, using historical home price data from the U.S. Census Bureau, we were able to spot a trend line. Our analysis shows that, over the past forty years, home prices in historically gay neighborhoods have steadily outperformed average prices for the metros in which they're located.

In the 1970s and '80s, some gay neighborhoods—like the Castro in San Francisco and Greenwich Village in New York City—were far cheaper than other parts of the city. In 1970, the average home in the Castro was 8.1 percent less expensive than the city on average. In 1980, home values in Greenwich Village were 5.4 percent below the city average. During a time of rampant homophobia, these neighborhoods became affordable and safe communities for gay men.

Then, over time, two things happened.

First, these communities gentrified. As Mickey Lauria of Clemson University and Lawrence Knopp of the University of Minnesota have pointed out, this happened in a two-step process. Low-income, LGBT populations moved to urban centers where rents were cheap—and where they could lead their lives free of judgment. Then, LGBT professionals followed in their footsteps, purchasing up housing stock and reinvesting in the neighborhood.

Second, the larger society slowly embraced gay rights and culture. Americans of every sexual orientation wanted to enjoy the culture, amenities, restaurants, and other exciting businesses in traditionally LGBT-friendly neighborhoods. By 2000, the Castro neighborhood boasted real estate prices that were nearly 40 percent *above* the average for the San Francisco metro. And home values in Greenwich Village had similarly soared to more than 27 percent greater than New York City as a whole.

The trend isn't universally applicable; some gay neighborhoods still lag behind the city average, especially in very expensive cities. But at the same time, the data *is* very clear. Many gay communities across the country are no longer marginalized and undervalued. As you can see in the chart on the next page, they're *coveted*.

The Andersonville neighborhood in Chicago serves as a powerful illustration of the wider transformation that's occurred in gay communities across America in recent decades. Andersonville is an

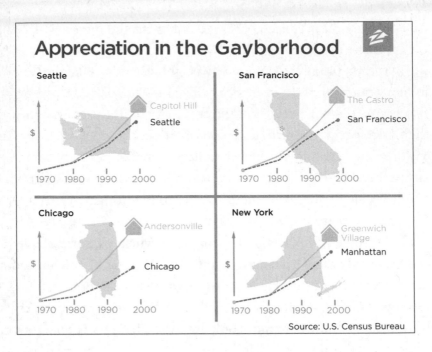

Appreciation in the Gayborhood

Seattle — Capitol Hill, Seattle — 1970 1980 1990 2000

San Francisco — The Castro, San Francisco — 1970 1980 1990 2000

Chicago — Andersonville, Chicago — 1970 1980 1990 2000

New York — Greenwich Village, Manhattan — 1970 1980 1990 2000

Source: U.S. Census Bureau

enclave in the larger, residential neighborhood of Edgewater, on Chicago's north side. During the 1970s, Andersonville property values hit relative rock bottom, as both the LGBT rights movement and a backlash of homophobia were on the rise. As a result, many LGBT people sought out low rents and strong community in the neighborhood. Over time, Andersonville became a place that was not just open to gays and lesbians, but where their culture became enmeshed with the larger civic culture. Gradually, more affluent LGBT people moved in, driving up real estate values even further. Now, Andersonville is one of the hottest neighborhoods in Chicago—so expensive that the original urban settlers no longer can afford to live there.

This pattern—across the country—is noteworthy for a number of reasons. For one thing, if you're looking for a home, you might want to consider up-and-coming LGBT-friendly neighborhoods—especially those that are located close to a Starbucks (for more, see Chapter 3). Note that your choices aren't limited to New York, Chicago, or San Francisco. We can see pockets of progress—both in terms of social tolerance and housing valuations—in areas of Albuquerque, El Paso, Fort Worth, Louisville, and Virginia Beach.[2]

But this pattern is also fascinating from another perspective. When you think about it, only a few years have passed since many politicians of both parties were calling for a constitutional amendment banning gay marriage, and a majority of Americans opposed gay rights. According to the Pew Research Center, 57 percent of the nation opposed gay marriage in 2001. Today, in 2014, only 39 percent are opposed, and 54 percent—an outright majority—are in favor of allowing same-sex marriage.[3] Prominent Republicans and President Obama have all come out in favor of gay rights. Celebrities across the pop culture spectrum have strongly endorsed marriage equality—including everyone from Brad Pitt and Angelina Jolie to the chart-topping rapper (and Seattle native) Macklemore.

This rapid about-face *feels* surprising. But, at least according to the data, it shouldn't be.

The housing data from recent decades shows that LGBT communities have become increasingly integrated into the American mainstream—much like other cultural and ethnic groups before them, and probably like many others to follow. We can plainly see America's advances on gay rights reflected in the data on home values. One might even argue that a process of LGBT migration, reinvestment, and community building in American cities was the crucial *precursor* to the significant social changes we're now experiencing.

Since the late 1960s and early 1970s, social scientists have aggregated and analyzed historic property transactions—preserved in deeds, titles, wills, and probate inventories—to resurrect and recreate a broader story about how American society has changed over time. Now, we can almost see these changes happening *in real time.*

No one doubts that social change can have a major impact on property values. But perhaps it's equally true that property values are a bellwether of social change...something to consider when weighing what the future holds—for our home values, and our nation's values, too.

Exterior of Hugh Hefner's Playboy Mansion *(Courtesy of Everett Collection)*

What's in a Street Name?

What Street Names Tell Us about Property Values

The 1930s were a confusing time to live in Arlington, Virginia.[1] You would make plans to meet a friend on Lincoln Avenue, and you'd wind up on opposite sides of town. That's because Arlington had at least *two* Lincoln Avenues, one in the north part of the city, and one in the south.

As the Arlington Public Library tells it, this wasn't the only case of repeated street names, and it was far from the most egregious. In fact, the county was crisscrossed with as many as twenty-five different streets called "Arlington." There were countless roads named "Washington," "Lee," and "Virginia." All over Arlington, street names were repeated, and the local population was becoming more and more mixed up.

This confusion was caused by an influx of residents that had more than tripled the county's population over the course of just thirty years. As Arlington grew from 6,430 in 1900 to 23,278 in 1930, housing developments sprang up all over town. There was no central planner to assign street names, so developers pretty much just went with their hearts—and they apparently didn't care whether they repeated a street name from the other side of town.

By 1932, this situation was becoming untenable. Businesses

were refusing to deliver packages to customers in Arlington for fear that their employees would get lost wandering the labyrinth of Arlington's roads, or make deliveries to the wrong address. The local fire department worried that they wouldn't be able to find burning homes without the most explicit directions. Visitors arrived in town and had no idea how to find their destinations.

The final straw came when the US Postal Service refused to establish a post office in Arlington until it sorted out its street-name situation. So, with that as motivation, Arlington County finally appointed a Street Naming Committee to re-title all of Arlington's roads. They set up a system of letters, numbers, and multi-syllable words—and within a year, the whole city was working to learn a new map of street names.

Arlington's example is unique, and not just because of the street-name chaos. It's very rare that a county will actually step back and reassign street names en masse. Instead, most of America's street names *still* reflect the whims of developers or whichever city planner happened to be in charge at the time…clarity be damned.

But here's the really interesting thing: This randomness has an unintended benefit. It actually packs street names with all kinds of information. Like fossils buried under layers of sand, street names capture essential facts about the homes on their blocks. That information has been buried for most of our history—but now we can finally uncover it.

We can tell, for instance, that a home on a street called "Lake" is probably worth an average of 70 percent more than the US median home value. If it's on "Cedar Court," that house was probably built around 1980 and has about eight other neighbors on its block. But a house on "Cedar Street?" That one was probably built in 1955.

What else can we tell? Well, when it comes to home value and street names, we can boil it down to a few simple maxims: First, names are better than numbers. Second, Lake Street beats Main Street. Third, suffixes matter.

NAMES ARE BETTER THAN NUMBERS

Let's take these rules one at a time. First, imagine two houses. Dave's house is on 10th Street, and Wendy's house is on Elm Street. With that piece of information alone, we can tell you that Wendy's house is probably worth more than Dave's. After all, homes on named streets tend to be more valuable than similar homes on numbered ones—an amazing 2 percent more valuable nationwide!

In some cities, the named-street premium is even higher than that national average. In Los Angeles, Philadelphia, Riverside, and San Francisco, the named-street premium clocks in at over 20 percent. A home on a named street in Dallas–Fort Worth is valued, on average, 4 percent more than a home on a numbered street.

The image on the next page shows the named-street premium in metro areas across the country. As you can see, we only found three places in the entire nation where named streets don't have the advantage. In Atlanta and New York, named and numbered streets come out roughly equal. Denver is the solitary example of a place where numbered streets are more valuable—probably because homes in its premier neighborhood of Country Club are located on numbered streets. East–west running streets in Country Club are numbered, while north–south streets are named. The same is true for other high home value Denver neighborhoods like Hilltop and Cherry Creek.

It's important to note here that we only looked at single-family residences in this analysis and throughout this chapter. That keeps large apartment complexes from skewing the data when we're looking at certain streets. Within this sample, we found that only 11 percent of single-family residences are located on numbered streets. The remaining 89 percent are all built on roads with a name.

Given the overwhelming preponderance of named streets, we decided to see what other information could be gleaned from the name of a road. In other words, we can finally answer that age-old question: What's in a name?

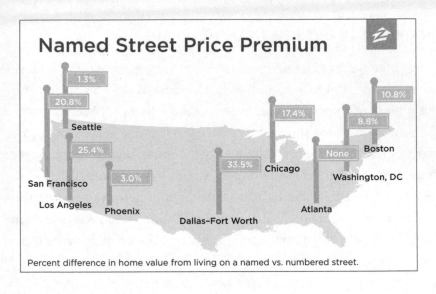

Percent difference in home value from living on a named vs. numbered street.

LAKE STREET BEATS MAIN STREET

Have you ever gone to a new town and noticed that it had all the same street names as the place where you live? You weren't imagining it. When we checked the data for the most common street names in America, the results were predictable. "Main Street" was by far the most common. After that, presidents, trees, and bodies of water dominated the list. Just look at this list of the fifteen most common American street names.

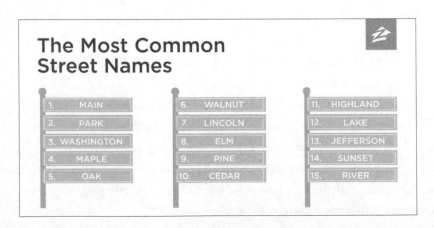

Main Streets across the country boast almost twice as many homes as their nearest competitor, but that doesn't make them valuable. In fact, it's just the opposite. If you live on Main Street, your home is probably worth around 4 percent less than America's median home value. It may be the most common, but Main Street is by far the least valuable of the most common road names.

On the other side of the spectrum, less common street names like "Lake" and "Sunset" are the clear winners in value. Homes on "Lake" on average are worth 16 percent more than the national average home value. "Sunset" houses are a close second, averaging 10 percent above the national median value.

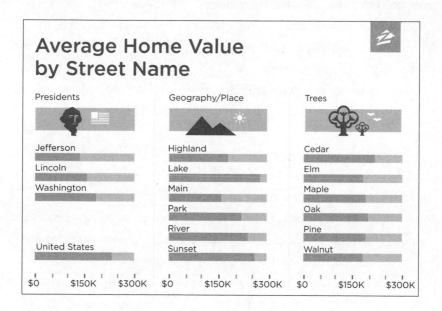

Now, we aren't recommending that you rush to city hall and start a petition to rename your street. Correlation, as every statistics class teaches, is not causation. Homes on "Lake" aren't valuable just because of the name; they're valuable because the descriptive name reflects a deeper truth about the real estate. In general, the most valuable street names describe something concrete about a home's location. It may be near the water, or at least have a terrific view of the sunset. This is why "Lake"—and other descriptive names like it—almost always beat "Main" in home value.

We did find one interesting exception to this rule: famous street names. In our houses, Bruce Springsteen and the Beatles are required listening. That must be true in a lot of homes, because these musicians have made an indelible mark on our country's music, our culture, and, apparently, our home values. If you're looking for a house on "Penny Lane," nationally you can expect to pay about $245,000—or 53 percent over the median home value as of mid-2013. Houses on "Thunder Road" are almost as expensive, averaging $234,000 nationwide—46 percent over the median value. Who says no one pays for music anymore?

(As with other market conditions, this varies locally, too. In Milwaukee and Boston, homes on "Thunder Road" are worth more than double the homes on "Penny Lane." Although the opposite is true in Sacramento and Riverside, California, where "Penny Lane" homes are twice as valuable as compared to "Thunder Road" homes.)

Of course, all of the numbers we've discussed so far reflect broad trends across the nation. As you've probably guessed, the picture gets more complicated as we zoom in on the local level. The most expensive streets vary enormously from place to place, as you can see from the image on the next page of the most valuable street names in major cities and their suburbs nationwide.

The names that are most common aren't usually the most valuable consistently across the nation. That's because valuable street names usually hint at the desirable characteristics in a given area. And those features are almost always locally specific.

For instance, it's no surprise that "Ocean" is the most valuable street in Miami and Boston, since those homes are near—you guessed it—the ocean. But in a city like Detroit, there's no reason "Ocean" would be a desirable place to live. There, it's much more valuable to live on "Lakeshore," since the area on the shore of Lake St. Clair is, arguably Detroit's finest. Of course, this isn't

Priciest Street Names

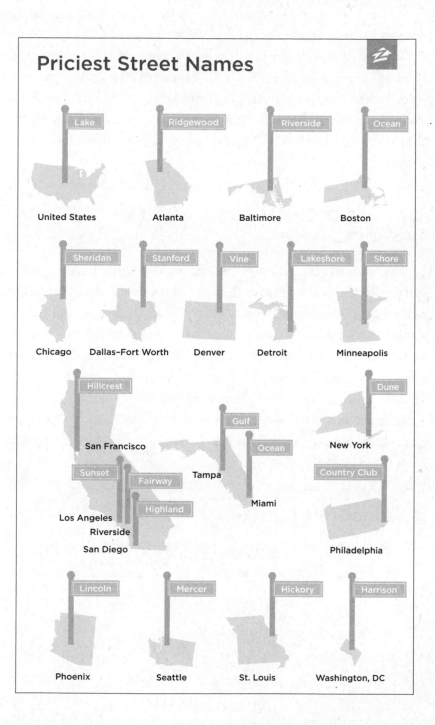

United States — Lake
Atlanta — Ridgewood
Baltimore — Riverside
Boston — Ocean
Chicago — Sheridan
Dallas–Fort Worth — Stanford
Denver — Vine
Detroit — Lakeshore
Minneapolis — Shore
San Francisco — Hillcrest
New York — Dune
Tampa — Gulf
Miami — Ocean
Los Angeles — Sunset
Riverside — Fairway
San Diego — Highland
Philadelphia — Country Club
Phoenix — Lincoln
Seattle — Mercer
St. Louis — Hickory
Washington, DC — Harrison

true for every street name. It's hard to say why "Hickory" is the place to be in St. Louis, or what "Vine" offers in Denver. But you won't need three guesses about why "Country Club" is the prime street to live on in the Philadelphia metro. The most valuable street names may vary from place to place, but the names almost always offer some clue about the features that make homes on that street so desirable. Or to put it another way: Lake Street beats Main Street.

ARE YOU BETTER OFF LIVING ON A LANE OR A BOULEVARD?

Of course, a street name has two parts: the name and the suffix. You might think it's an afterthought whether a road is labeled as a "street," a "boulevard," or a "drive." But, in fact, we found that homes on "Washington *Street*" are often very different from homes on "Washington *Court*." National distribution of street suffixes is fairly instinctual. "Streets" and "drives" are the most common. "Places" and "boulevards" are the rarest.

Like the first part of the street name, the decision of which suffix to choose is left mostly to the whims of the entity that builds

All about Suffixes

Suffix	% of Homes	Average Home Value	Average Year of Construction	Average # of Homes per Street
Avenue	16%	$233,350	1956	15
Boulevard	1%	$271,980	1968	28
Circle	4%	$252,510	1986	13
Court	9%	$278,060	1988	9
Drive	23%	$245,450	1980	18
Lane	8%	$270,500	1983	9
Place	4%	$306,780	1976	13
Road	11%	$240,870	1970	13
Street	17%	$183,120	1955	18
Way	4%	$312,500	1986	14

the street. And again, this winds up imbuing the street suffix with more information than you might expect. The "trails," "loops," and "coves" are more rare. Just like baby names, different street suffixes were in vogue at different points in time. So while "streets" and "avenues" were all the rage in the 1950s, the late 1980s was the age of "ways," "circles," and "courts."

We can also use street suffixes to predict how many neighbors a home has. "Boulevards" and "avenues" contain the most homes, while "courts" and "lanes" contain the fewest homes, on average.

Perhaps most significantly, suffixes offer a great deal of insight into home values. When we crunched the numbers on home values and street names, we found a direct connection between street suffix and the value of a home.

The most common names tend to be the least valuable. In this case, the four most common street suffixes for homes are the four least valuable suffixes. On the flip side, "way" and "place" are the most valuable suffixes, even though they each make up only a meager 4 percent of suffixes nationwide.

Here, too, this national data becomes much more complicated once we zoom in on the local level. In some metro areas, the value of homes with particular suffixes closely mirrors the national data. If we look at Phoenix, for instance, the suffix patterns are fairly similar to the national trends.

Even as local patterns vary, one fact is fairly consistent. "Street" is almost always *one of* the lowest-valued common suffixes, if not *the* lowest. In fifteen out of the top twenty metropolitan areas, houses with "street" as a suffix are valued lower than the majority of other suffixes in the metro. For example, in Detroit, "street" is the most common street suffix for homes—but it also carries the lowest home values by far.

Of course, this rule—like all others—has some exceptions. A noteworthy one is Washington, DC, where "street" is one of the most expensive suffixes by average home value. In this case, it's probably because many of the Georgetown homes of senators, ambassadors, and Washington power brokers—some of Washington's most expensive real estate—have "street" as a suffix.

So here's a tip for developers building a new subdivision: Suffixes matter. Steer clear of "streets" and "roads," and stick with "ways," "places," and "courts" instead.

HOW YOUR STREET GOT ITS NAME

Street names often seem, well, totally random—especially if you're visiting a friend's neighborhood on the other side of town, or traveling in a new city for the first time. But there is a method to the street-naming madness. So we spoke to a Tampa-area developer to find out how the process works when a new parcel of land is being built up.

First, the developer scopes out the area to see how streets in surrounding communities are named. Then, more often than not, the developer picks a theme for the new community and its yet-to-be-named streets—like, for instance, "Caribbean," or "Equestrian," or "Presidents of the US." With a theme in mind, the developer puts together a list of preferred names. (The company we spoke with even holds contests for employees to suggest names—if an employee's submission eventually makes it onto a street sign, he or she gets a prize.) The list is submitted to the county or municipality, which cross-checks it against a list of existing streets for any names that sound similar, so as not to inadvertently confuse emergency personnel. And then, with the local government's stamp of approval, the street-naming process is complete.

Interior of the set of Monica and Rachel's living room from the TV show *Friends*
(Courtesy Everett Collection)

20

Empire Real Estate of Mind

Analyzing the Oddities of New York City

New York, NY. Some call it "the city so great they named it twice." We call it "the real estate market so exceptional that it needs its own chapter."

Real estate in the Empire State is close to my (Spencer's) heart. I grew up in Manhattan and my mother was a real estate agent. As a kid, my parents would drag me to open houses, and I now return the favor to my own children. I know firsthand just how odd the New York real estate market is, and not just because it's so expensive.

New York City—and we're talking about the city now, not the metro region, which is very different—has different fundamentals and different rules, so it's no surprise that its real estate market functions very differently than pretty much anywhere else in America. Think back to the ways in which gentrification patterns were influenced by New York being a collection of islands.

Regardless of what dataset we look at, New York City is there, like some gigantic black hole, warping the data in fascinating ways that we're just beginning to understand. As the Rolling Stones sing, "Go ahead, bite the Big Apple, don't mind the maggots."[1] So we'll take a cue from one of our favorite songs and take a bite out of the Big Apple's housing peculiarities.

New York City's housing exceptionalism begins with its land—
or, rather, with what little of it there is. Together, the city's five
boroughs cover 302.6 square miles, with an astonishing 27,012
people packed into each and every one of them. In Manhattan,
New York's densest borough, there are a mindboggling 69,467
people per square mile. By contrast, the population density of the
United States as a whole is a roomy 87 people per square mile. In
other words, Manhattan is almost *eight hundred times denser* than
the rest of the country—no wonder you practically have to suck in
your stomach just to walk down the streets of Manhattan.

All of New York's distinctive housing features follow more
or less from that single fact. As you'll no doubt remember from
your high school economics class, limited supply means greater
demand for each unit, which in turn drives up prices. Historically, US home prices have averaged about two-and-a-half times
Americans' incomes, with homeowners putting one-fifth of their
incomes toward mortgages. But in the New York metro area, it's
not unusual for home prices to be four or more times greater than
annual incomes, and mortgage payments typically gobble up nearly
one-third of New Yorkers' annual income—exceeding the federal
government's standard definition of what constitutes "affordable"
housing.

The median sale price per square foot of homes in the New
York metro region—which includes everything from Long Island,
to Newark, to Bridgeport, Connecticut—is double the US median.
Homes within the city itself sell for *nearly four times more*. And in
Manhattan, New York's smallest—and densest—borough, home
prices are more than ten times what they are in the rest of the
country.

Not only is New York housing expensive, it also varies greatly
by micro-neighborhood. The city's five boroughs are comprised of
fifty-nine community districts (what we usually refer to as neighborhoods, but these are quite large), and hundreds of smaller neighborhoods.[2] Home values are tied to these neighborhoods—and can

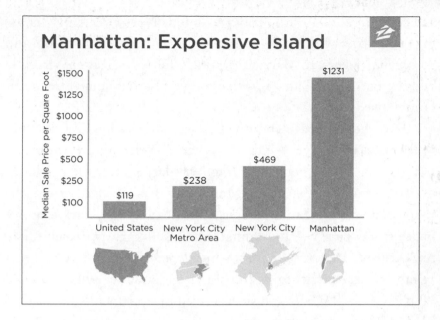

often differ dramatically over the course of just a few blocks. In 2013, for example, two equally nice East Village apartments were listed on Zillow. Both were renovated two-bedroom, one-bath units, and both boasted 1,000 square feet of living space (that's a very nice-sized apartment, by New York standards).[3] They were both a stone's throw from Tompkins Square Park and right around the corner from each other, a three-minute walk apart at most. And yet the difference between asking prices was $200,000. This is typical in New York, given the diversity of housing to be found on any given block, and relative access to subway or bus lines.

With homes so hard to afford, the rate of homeownership in New York is as low as Manhattan's skyscrapers are high. From 2008 to 2012, less than one-third of New Yorkers own their own home.[4] In the Bronx, just 20 percent own their home. During the same period, you'll recall, the national figure was 66 percent—and that still isn't high enough for the policy makers who see homeownership as the central pillar of the American Dream.

New York may be the quintessentially American city, but not when it comes to owning homes, or when it comes to the housing stock itself. With so little room to build, New York City's housing stock overwhelmingly consists of "multi-family" condo and co-op apartments. In Manhattan, single-family homes are virtually nonexistent. More than *98 percent* of Manhattan homes are multi-family dwellings.[5]

If we burrow further into that iconic borough, we see that Manhattan epitomizes—indeed, is driving—the rapid transformation of New York's housing market writ large. Over the centuries, in fact, the very texture of Manhattan has changed, from the shape of its coastline to the height of its homes. Nineteenth-century brownstones gave way to Manhattan's first luxury apartments, like the exclusive Dakota building, which opened in 1894. Tenements began adding electric stoves and hot water, and, by the 1930s, a full 90 percent of Manhattan residents lived in apartments.

In some cases, these were Art Deco masterpieces like the San Remo, which a 1930 advertisement in the *New York Times* called "as modern as a flying boat, as luxurious as the Île de France, and designed for people who are at home on both. Birds in the sky are your only neighbors."[6] Others lived in the flat, drab, brick-and-glass apartments that were standard in the postwar era.

Particularly popular was "cooperative" housing, pioneered in the late nineteenth century[7] and currently comprising roughly three-quarters of Manhattan's housing stock.[8] Co-ops, like many aspects—and people—of New York, are pretty strange. Co-op owners technically don't own real estate; they own shares in a corporation that owns real estate. Prospective residents must be approved by a powerful, independent co-op board—often operating like an exclusive yet byzantine country club—and neither owner names nor sale prices were made public until a 2006 law mandated disclosure. As of today, information on square footage and the numbers of bedrooms and bathrooms is still not made public.

But whether the buildings Manhattanites moved into were co-ops or condos, postmodern or the popular prewar buildings unique to the city, more and more people flooded into the borough, until their neighbors were not just birds in the sky, but the 1.7 million other Manhattan residents sharing their small patch of earth.

Today, New York developers operate with their heads in the clouds—literally. While home builders in most places concern themselves with buying land and rights of way, Manhattan real estate titans jockey for the "air rights" to build their residential towers. (The concept of air rights dates back to a nifty medieval Roman law declaring, "whoever owns the soil, it is theirs up to Heaven and down to Hell.") They build up—because there's nowhere else to build.

That's how we have come to marvel at feats of engineering like the striking, sinuous Gehry Tower, at 8 Spruce Street, whose 870 feet recently supplanted Donald Trump's 861-foot Trump World Tower—for now—as the tallest all-residential building in New York. The base of the mixed-use Gehry building holds a public elementary school and retail stores, while the remainder of its seventy-six glass stories houses nearly nine hundred residential units.

One of these Gehry units, an $11,300/month three-bedroom posted on Zillow, featured a "honey colored critical grain appointed kitchen with top of the line stainless steel appliances," in a building with "indoor and outdoor amenity spaces including a 50-foot swimming pool with sky lit space, a wraparound sundeck, state of the art fitness center with a view of the Brooklyn Bridge and a spa treatment suite with private treatment rooms, a group fitness studio as well as yoga and Pilates, with private training studios and lastly bike storage."[9] (We hasten to note the effectiveness of the well-written listing! For more on crafting *your* listing, please see Chapter 11.) From these castles in the clouds, well-heeled Manhattanites will be able to look out over the half-dozen new residential buildings, such as the One57 tower and 432 Park Avenue, which, at over 1,000 feet tall, already surpass 8 Spruce in height—as well as the frenzied construction that has begun spreading to Brooklyn and Queens.[10]

Of course, not just anyone can afford these apartments. These high-priced high-rises are driving out many of the city's lower- and middle-income residents, contributing to what Spike Lee famously called "Christopher Columbus Syndrome." As the filmmaker wrote in March, 2014:

> The Truth is Gentrification is Great for the New Arrivals in Harlem, South Bronx, Bushwick, Red Hook, Bed-Stuy Do or Die and Fort Greene, and in many other cities across the U.S. But not so great for The Brown and Black Residents who have been in these Neighborhoods for decades and are being forced out, to the Suburbs, Down South or back to their Native Islands.[11]

What's more, illegal evictions are all too common, and rent-controlled apartments—units with tenants living continuously from before July 1, 1971, for which landlords are limited in how much they can raise the rent—are disappearing. Every year, Manhattan loses more than ten thousand low-cost apartments as properties leave the rent stabilization program.[12] How does this work? Landlords eager to cash in tend to renovate newly vacant apartments, lifting their rents above the city's regulation threshold of $2,500 a month, and thereby removing them from the stabilization rolls.[13] The few "affordable" apartments left often are cramped and undesirable places to live.

Replacing longtime residents is a new urban elite. Because Manhattan is a world economic center, home to many cultural amenities such as museums, galleries, and music as well as many world-renowned restaurants and luxury shops, New York City attracts an exceptionally large number of foreign buyers. Using Zillow traffic data from May 2013, we see that—notwithstanding the trophy properties that are being snatched up by wealthy Russians and Chinese[14, 15]—Canadians and Brits are actually the foreigners flocking in greatest numbers to New York City.

At the same time, New York has become ever more dependent

on the financial sector's big-time bonus culture. In 2000, more than 35 percent of the wages from the city's earners came from Wall Street—nearly triple what it was in 1970.[16] The *New York Times* estimated that in 2006—despite former mayor Michael Bloomberg's hope of reducing the city's reliance on this one industry—the 280,000 workers in the finance industry took home more than half of all the wages paid in Manhattan.[17]

What this means is that New York home prices have become inextricably linked to what happens in Manhattan. After the planes hit the Twin Towers on 9/11, Manhattan condo prices fell 2.6 percent, and the volume of sales fell, too. Major government subsidies and incentives quickly helped restore property values and transform the Financial District, as one headline proclaimed, "from rubble to renaissance."[18] By July 2002, Manhattan condo prices surpassed their pre-9/11 peak.

Six years later, the collapse of Lehman Brothers and the beginning of the 2008 financial crisis took a more lasting toll on the market. Credit was tight; the financial industry that drove so much of the market was in free fall. As the table above illustrates, Manhattan home values peaked in March 2008—later than those in the United States and the New York metro area—the same month JPMorgan Chase and the Federal Reserve attempted to bail out Bear Stearns (incidentally, a former employer of Spencer's). The peak exactly coincides with the month in which Bear Stearns shareholders approved the firm's sale to JPMorgan Chase. Despite being two to five times higher, Manhattan home values declined much less sharply from their peak when compared to home values in the other four boroughs.

After dropping 18.2 percent from March 2008 to November 2009, home values in Manhattan have rebounded. The financial industry that drove the luxury housing market has been somewhat replaced by the purchasing power of foreign buyers, as banks cut down on bonuses and co-op boards remain reluctant to bring on finance professionals.

We see, then, a city growing faster, higher, and denser, as home values go through the ceiling—and through the ceiling again. We also see a city marked by widening economic chasms befitting its immense urban canyons. Consider the fact that income inequality in Manhattan is roughly the same as in Swaziland, the sub-Saharan nation replete with both gated mansions and endless cardboard shantytowns—a country the World Bank ranks as the twentieth most financially *unequal* on Earth.[19]

Of course, New York is hardly alone in this sense. Unaffordable housing has fueled dissent and demonstrations in cities from Paris, to London, to San Francisco (where many have expressed their outrage over rapidly rising rents by protesting the private fleets of shuttle buses that whisk tech-company employees from downtown homes to Silicon Valley offices).

Sooner or later, all of these trends may come to a head, with ripple effects throughout American politics and culture. After all, New Yorkers' frustration with skyrocketing housing costs helped propel the progressive Bill de Blasio from the back of the Democratic-primary pack to Gracie Mansion during the city's 2013 mayoral campaign. Most observers think New York's real estate market is an island untethered from national trends, but when it comes to a leftward lean in American urban politics, New York could be something of a canary in the coal mine.

Ultimately, what happens next is anyone's guess. But in the near term, this much is clear: New York and its equivalents are experiencing an urban revival in many ways, becoming the new incubators for innovative ideas and cutting-edge culture. And yet the less affluent are retreating to the suburbs, as the Manhattans of the world become more and more isolated, "patrician ghettos"[20] of luxury and inequality.

Exterior of Southfork Ranch, the Ewing family home from the TV show *Dallas* (*Courtesy Everett Collection*)

The Wild, Wild West

America's Most Volatile Housing Markets

We've all seen the bumper sticker—"Virginia Is for Lovers." But the one we keep looking for is the one that reads, "Arizona is for Volatility Lovers." And it's not just Arizona. To live in the "Sand States" is to make your home in a place with abundant sunshine and even more abundant price fluctuation.

During the housing recession, a well-informed person simply couldn't discuss the housing crisis without mentioning three cities: Las Vegas, Phoenix, or Riverside, California.

The national media seemed to be in a competition to label these cities the ground zero of the housing crisis. "Stuck in Phoenix, the Epicenter of Housing Crisis,"[1] read one MarketWatch headline. The Utah *Standard-Examiner* ran a story titled, "How Las Vegas became the epicenter of the housing crisis."[2] While the UK's *Guardian* ran, "A housing crisis tour of Riverside."[3] A new shorthand term even emerged to describe Arizona, California, and Nevada—along with Florida. They were grouped together and branded the "Sand States," because apparently someone noticed that they had a few things in common: deserts, beaches, and remarkably volatile housing markets.

In time, it became a given that these markets were just, well, *different* from others.

By now you know that we love deflating myths. So you might

be surprised to hear us affirm that this actually is one of those rare cases where the conventional wisdom got it completely right. These three housing markets really *are* different from other ones across the United States—and not just during these tumultuous recent years. Las Vegas, Phoenix, and Riverside have been unpredictable throughout their history, and they remain incredibly volatile even as the national housing market recovers.

This doesn't necessarily mean you shouldn't buy a home in these cities. In fact, these places have a lot to recommend them. But being a homeowner in one of these three markets is not for the faint of heart. When it comes to housing, it turns out that these Western markets are still very wild, indeed.

THREE VOLATILE MARKETS

We can measure volatility in a number of ways, but the best way to start is simply by looking at how much local home values change from quarter to quarter. That means we disregard whether the value change is up or down, and instead pay attention to the magnitude of value swings over time.

We ran the numbers since 1985—nationwide—and, sure enough, Phoenix, Riverside, and Las Vegas are three of the largest, most unstable housing markets in the country. In Riverside, home values change by an average of 2.9 percent every single quarter. In Las Vegas, housing prices swing an average of 2.6 percent each quarter. In Phoenix, that number is 2.4 percent. (In contrast Pittsburgh—which is one of the most stable markets in the country—sees an average quarterly change of only 1.2 percent.)

If anything, these averages actually underrepresent just how much home values can shift in a single quarter in the Wild, Wild West. In Phoenix, home values have appreciated by as much as 15 percent in a single quarter. That's right, *in a single quarter*. But they've also dropped as low as -8 percent in that same time frame. Quarterly home value appreciation in Riverside has been as high as

11 percent and as low as -10 percent. Las Vegas has seen the highest quarterly home appreciation, 18 percent, but it has also seen appreciation drop as low as -13 percent.

Compared to these peaks and valleys, Pittsburgh's home values practically appear to be a vast flatland. Across this same time period, Pittsburgh's maximum quarterly home value appreciation was only 4.8 percent. And the quarterly change in the metropolitan area's home values has not dropped below 2.3 percent in almost thirty years!

LIVING WITH VOLATILITY

Now, this all may sound a little abstract. Of course the housing crisis was a nightmare, but really, what's the difference whether quarterly home values are increasing 3 percent or 1 percent? Does that really affect a person's life?

To get a sense of what it feels like to be a homeowner in these markets, imagine the experience of buying a home in one. It's a moment of nervous excitement. You start looking at paint samples and furniture. You invite friends over to check out the backyard. This might even be the place where you start your family and spend the rest of your life.

If you buy a home in Phoenix, Riverside, or Las Vegas, all of those feelings are still there, of course. But it turns out there's probably something else that's in the back of your mind—or should be: You have no idea whether this house will be worth anywhere close to what you paid for it in five years.

For all you know, the value could plummet. In fact, if you bought a home in Riverside between 1985 and 2013, the odds that you would lose money on your house over any five-year period were *almost even* with the odds that you'd make money!

When most people buy a home, they see it as a measure of certainty in their lives. *When people in these three Wild West markets buy homes, they should think of it as a coin flip.*

Even if you're buying a home with a thirty-year mortgage—and are planning to stay in it for all thirty of those years—you still care about the shifts in value. How big are those shifts in the Wild West? Well, to give you a better sense of the scale, we broke down the value shifts over a series of five-year periods from 1985 to 2013.

First, let's look at our stable market, Pittsburgh, just to get a sense of what a less volatile market looks like. During the last three decades, buying a home there was nothing like a trip to a casino. In fact, if you bought a home in the Steel City any time between 1985 and 2013, you would have always—yes, always—experienced a gain in home value over five years.

In contrast, a home buyer in Las Vegas experienced a loss in home value after five years 18 percent of the time. In Phoenix, homeowners experienced a value loss 27 percent of the time. In Riverside, a home buyer suffered a loss an astonishing *40 percent* of the time!

The magnitude of these losses is enormous. The *worst* five-year period of homeownership in Pittsburgh saw the homeowner still gaining 2 percent in home value after their purchase. But in Riverside and Phoenix, the worst five-year performance saw a 54 percent decline in home values. In Las Vegas, the worst five years came with a whopping 62 percent decline.

Of course, the flip side is also true: When times have been good, these volatile markets have performed significantly better than their more stable counterparts. Pittsburgh's best five years saw home values gaining a respectable 35 percent. But during the Wild West markets' best five years, homes in Phoenix gained 118 percent. Homes in Las Vegas went up 126 percent in value. And home values in Riverside nearly tripled, rising 184 percent.

Once again, however, it's interesting to note that the *average* five-year performances in the Wild West and stable Pittsburgh are actually pretty similar: 22 percent up for both Pittsburgh and Phoenix, 24 percent up for Vegas, and 35 percent up for Riverside. In other words, despite the roller-coaster ride in the three Wild West markets, their average performance generally mirrored the slow but steady upward trajectory in Pittsburgh.

There's an analogy here to the game of blackjack. You might get some fantastic hands, and you might have some terrific blowups. But if you play absolutely perfectly, over time, you and the house might come out just about even.

It's still a gamble, though—and sometimes you lose big. For the people who bought at the wrong moment, it doesn't matter that they eventually might enjoy a similar appreciation to Pittsburgh. They've been hit with enormous home value declines, and they're underwater *right now.*

In fact, the level of negative equity in Las Vegas was among the worst in the nation as of the second quarter of 2013. Some 48 percent of Vegas homeowners with a mortgage are in negative equity. Almost 13 percent of homeowners owe *twice as much* on their mortgage as the current value of their home. And even more people are in effective negative equity, which means they have less than 20 percent equity in their homes. Even if they are not technically underwater, their tiny amount of equity means that they won't be able to sell for enough to pay off the mortgage while covering the fees and down payments on a new home. They're essentially under house arrest—and it's their house that's holding them captive.

On top of that, all of this negative equity actually makes the local housing market *even more* volatile. As a result of homeowners in negative equity trapped in their homes, the supply of available housing in these markets decreases, leading to price spikes as potential buyers are forced to compete for a smaller pool of homes. The cycle of volatility leads to even more volatility.

You can see why it's so troubling that almost 67 percent of Las Vegas homeowners are in true or effective negative equity. When two-thirds of Las Vegas homeowners with a mortgage can't afford to move to another home, it's devastating for those homeowners, and it's terrible for the local housing market. It's just one more unfortunate side effect of the unpredictable home markets in the Wild West.

WHY THE WEST IS WILD

By now you're probably wondering: Where does all this volatility come from?

There are a lot of complicated answers to that simple question. Partly, these markets are volatile because they have high employment flexibility. They're the kind of places people can move to and find work when times are good. But they also tend to be the kind of places that empty out when the jobs aren't there.

As you can see from this graph, the labor markets in these three cities are far more volatile than in other parts of the country. There are various explanations for this stemming from local conditions. Las Vegas, for instance, is unusually dependent on consumer spending, a fickle basis for an economy.[4]

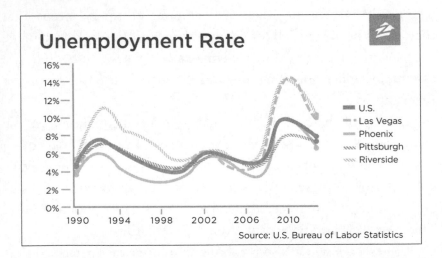

These unstable unemployment rates are directly connected with housing prices. And that stands to reason, because local workers all need somewhere to live. When times are good and jobs are plentiful, the number of households—*i.e.*, occupied homes—goes through the roof, as it were. Families show up and buy up the available housing stock, which drives up the prices of the homes that remain. It's basic supply and demand—and in these places, both supply and demand are influenced by inherently volatile factors.

Look at Riverside, for instance. At one point in 1989, the number of households in the city was increasing at five times the national rate. But fewer than four years later, that trend was turned

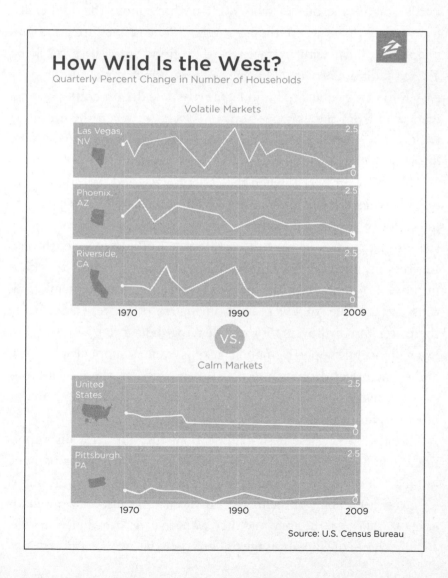

How Wild Is the West?
Quarterly Percent Change in Number of Households

Volatile Markets

Las Vegas, NV — 2.5 — 0

Phoenix, AZ — 2.5 — 0

Riverside, CA — 2.5 — 0

1970   1990   2009

VS.

Calm Markets

United States — 2.5 — 0

Pittsburgh, PA — 2.5 — 0

1970   1990   2009

Source: U.S. Census Bureau

on its head. By 1993, Riverside's growth was down to about two-thirds of that of the rest of the country. When we crunched the data, we found that Riverside's household change rate is actually four times more volatile than that of the rest of the United States. It's no wonder that the supply and demand dynamics tend to be volatile there, too.

It's also not a coincidence that the "Sand States" all have warm weather year-round. They tend to be magnets for retirees and second-home buyers who want nothing more than a beautiful, warm climate where they can relax. When times are good and people are flush with extra cash, they flood into these markets. There's a lot of open space in these places, which makes it relatively easy for new residents to build expansive new dream homes instead of buying from the existing housing stock. So when the economy is booming, these markets tend to fill up with home buyers who drive up demand—and drive home prices through the roof.

This all seems great when the economy is good, but it goes bad quickly when the economy falters. When times are bad, it's hard to find a lot of snowbirds who are willing to fork over the money for the ultimate extravagance: an extra home in the sunny Southwest. Retirees on fixed incomes probably aren't going to make this kind of move at a time when the market is suffering. And remember all those extra homes that were built during the boom years? Suddenly there aren't many buyers for them, leaving the market with a glut of excess housing supply. Demand slackens even as supply is plentiful, and home prices drop as a result. Taken together, these conditions create a dynamic in which every national economic hiccup is multiplied several times over in these markets.

What's more, these desirable locations also attract a disproportionate number of foreign buyers. These people have the same basic mind-set: They want a vacation home, either to use or to rent out as an investment. Some of them even buy homes because they have kids going to college in the area, and they want to give them a place to live.

We checked Zillow's usage data to see who was shopping in the

Wild West, and we found that 42 percent of people shopping Zillow for Phoenix homes from abroad are Canadians. Another 15 percent are from India, Australia, and the United Kingdom (close to 5 percent each).

Riverside is also among the most popularly searched places by Canadian, Chinese, Indian, British, and Mexican Zillow users. Canadians again make up the largest group of foreigners searching for homes in Riverside, accounting for 28.6 percent of foreigners searching in the metro area. Chinese users are the next biggest group, making up 6 percent of searches in May 2013.

And in Las Vegas, Canadians again constitute the greatest percentage of foreign shoppers: 25 percent. They're followed by British users (6.7 percent) and Chinese users (4.8 percent).

Just like the retirees and the second-home buyers, these foreign home buyers bring inherent instability into the market. They can be driven to buy more homes when times are good—or retreat entirely—due to economic factors on the other side of the world (or at least the other side of the 49th parallel). Once again, every small event, however distant, is amplified in these Wild Western housing markets.

Ironically, these three housing markets are cursed by their own desirability. They attract a lot of people, yes, but not the steady supply of homeowners and buyers who keep markets like Pittsburgh relatively steady and safe for home buyers. Instead, transitory workers, retirees, and foreign investors are together responsible for keeping the West wild.

Does this mean you should avoid living in Phoenix, Riverside, or Las Vegas? Not necessarily. There are plenty of people who swear they wouldn't want to live anywhere else. You might, in fact, be among them.

But if you're going to buy a house in one of these markets, expect a significant amount of short- and medium-term ups and downs. Don't assume that a booming market is going to continue. And remember that any national or global trend has the potential to destabilize your local market.

Archie Bunker's family in their living room from the TV show *All in the Family* (CBS/Photofest)

22

Statistics Are People, Too

*Looking at the Housing Bust in More
than Just Dollars and Cents*

As executives and economists, we have a favorite saying: "Statistics are just people with the tears wiped off." After all, when the experts and pundits talk about the housing collapse, they're all too quick to forget that behind the numbers are real people who felt real impact—people who lost their homes, their jobs, their life savings. And since the housing bubble burst in 2007, we have paid close attention to news reports about the hardships people have suffered in its wake. Too many have been unforgettable.

The housing market crash and ensuing recession—the worst since the Great Depression—upended millions of lives. And for every news report of individual hardship and loss since the housing bubble burst, countless more stories have gone untold. So, to help us better understand the impact of the housing market crash on human beings, we turned to survey data from Gallup, some of which is used to construct the Gallup-Healthways Well-Being Index, a daily measure of Americans' health and well-being.

During January 2008, well-being company Healthways partnered with Gallup to combine their decades of respective expertise in polling, health research, and behavioral economics. Together, they created "an in-depth, real-time view of Americans' well-being." Since then, they have surveyed more than two million American adults, asking respondents about a range of topics—from their personal finances, to their outlook on their community and social relationships, to their general physical and emotional health—to compute the Well-Being Index. By comparing this data to housing market data, we stumbled upon several interesting and, we believe, significant ways in which the performance of the real estate market has corresponded to the overall health and well-being of Americans.

One thing we spotted right away is a strong relationship between the performance of the housing market and Gallup's measure of Americans' level of optimism about the economy. As you would expect, as the housing market declined, optimism about the economy plummeted, too. And as the housing market began turning around, optimism trended back upward. In January 2008, before the economy began its rapid downslide, the survey data shows that 18 percent of Americans were optimistic that the economy was improving. As the housing market continued to get worse over the next five months, optimism about the economy declined, too. By May 2008, it had dropped to an all-time low of 8 percent. That means in just five months, 24 million people lost their optimism about the economy. That's a group of people practically the size of Texas.

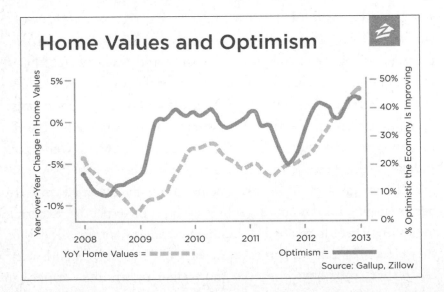

Home Values and Optimism

Source: Gallup, Zillow

Of course, the housing market was far from the only factor affecting people's optimism about the economy. In the roller coaster of peaks and plummets of public economic optimism, we can easily spot some of the biggest headlines from the past five years. For example, when the $787 billion American Recovery and Reinvestment Act was signed into law in February 2009, it corresponded with an increase in economic optimism. Then, in the summer of 2011—right around the time of the so-called "debt ceiling" crisis, when Washington spooked the markets by threatening not to authorize the government's ability to borrow more money—we see a dip in economic optimism. Other economic factors—such as the price of fuel or the unemployment rate—surely played a role in influencing optimism, too.

It's important to note that there's no way to know whether rising optimism was a *cause* of the increase in housing prices (i.e., people saying, "Things are getting better, let's go shopping for a new home!") or a *consequence* of it (i.e., people saying, "Look, housing prices are rising, so things must be getting better!"). Like the fabled chicken and egg, we're not sure which came first. But even putting aside other economic factors, it's clear that the performance of the housing market can provide unique insight into Americans' overall economic confidence, and the interrelationship between the two is a strong one.

We also found that the performance of the housing market is linked to Americans' general outlook on life. The Well-Being Index survey measures this by asking respondents where they picture themselves on a ten-step ladder (also known as the Cantril Self-Anchoring Striving Scale), with the top step of the ladder representing the best possible life they could be living, and the floor representing the worst possible life. People who imagine themselves on the seventh step or above now, and the eighth step or above in the future, are considered to be "thriving." Those who see themselves on or below the fourth step are considered to be "suffering."

In January 2008, before the economy began its rapid downslide, 60 percent of respondents saw themselves on the seventh step or above. But by November 2008, as the housing market took a sharp turn for the worse, those in the "thriving" category dropped to below 50 percent. This decrease amounted to just over 24 million adults—or the populations of the New York and Boston metro regions combined.

From January to December 2008, the percentage of survey respondents reporting that they were smiling on any given day dropped roughly 2 percent. That means about 4.8 million people were smiling less on any given day at the end of the year than they had been at the beginning. On top of that, fewer people answered "yes" to the question "Did you experience happiness a lot of the day yesterday?"

All of that emotional stress took a physical toll. Real estate agents like to joke that you can tell how long a house has been on the market by looking at the seller's nails—if they're bitten down, the house has been on the market for too long.

The same idea holds true on a much larger scale, as well. By comparing the Well-Being Index to Zillow data, we can see a strong association between how the housing market is performing and Americans' blood pressure and cholesterol levels. The data shows that market declines are accompanied by increases in both blood pressure and cholesterol levels.

As the economy worsened over the course of 2008, the number of respondents reporting ever having high cholesterol levels increased from just under 29 percent to a little more than 30 percent. That might not sound like an enormous leap, but that means 2.5 million people—the equivalent of the Miami metro area—saw their cholesterol jump as 2008 went on. The percentage of Americans reporting ever having high blood pressure rose a full percentage point as well, to more than 27 percent.

Finally, these trends began to reverse themselves as the economy recovered. As more and more homes began increasing in value in mid-2011, the percentage of respondents reporting ever having high blood pressure and cholesterol levels began to come down, to 25.5 percent and 29.5 percent, respectively.

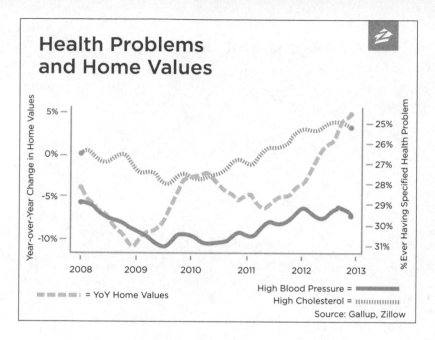

Blood pressure and cholesterol weren't the only things peaking as the market bottomed out; cigarette smoking skyrocketed as well. The reality is that increased cigarette smoking is tied to increased stress levels, and there was plenty to be stressed about as home prices plummeted and unemployment mounted. In January 2008, 20.7 percent of Americans surveyed said they smoked. By December of the same year, 22.2 percent said they did. That's a new smoking population just under the size of the city of Los Angeles. And that increased smoking, in turn, may have played a role in all that elevated blood pressure and cholesterol.

When we focus on specific metro areas, we're able to get an even more detailed picture of the ways in which the housing market's performance is linked to Americans' health and well-being. Not surprisingly, the more that housing values have fallen from their peak prices in a given area (that is to say, the bigger the housing bubble has burst in local markets), the bigger the change has been in people's lives and livelihoods. In metros that experienced

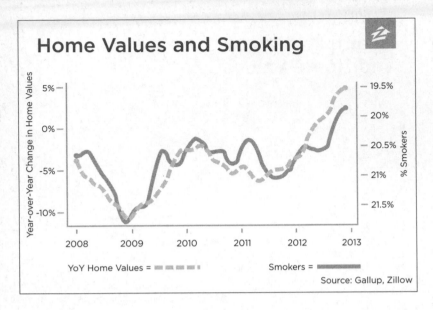

the furthest falls from peak, the Well-Being Index showed higher percentages of people reporting that they were in poor health and that they'd personally struggled to provide shelter for themselves or their family. People living in these areas were less likely also to report experiencing happiness and more likely to report experiencing sadness. When asked where they saw themselves on the ten-step ladder, fewer said they were currently at or above the seventh step, and more said they were on or below the fourth. It's not surprising that people in these hard-hit metros were also more likely to describe the overall economy as suffering, too.

When we looked at metro areas with *above average* rates of negative equity, we saw a similar story. Many homeowners in these communities stomach the nauseating task of writing a monthly mortgage check to pay off a home that's worth less than they bought it for, month after month, and thus feel themselves sliding further and further away from financial security. Fewer people in these metros feel good about the amount of money they have to spend, and they tend to be less satisfied with their own standard of living. Additionally, residents of these metros tend to score lower

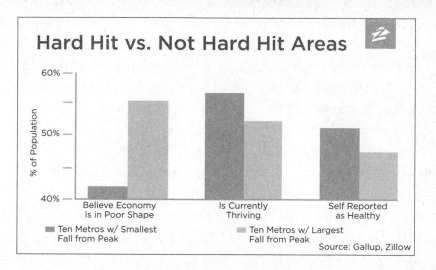

on the basic access index, which measures whether people have a safe place to live and everyday necessities like food and health care. It's no wonder people in these metros are more likely to assign the economy a bad grade.

All this leads us to one more measure—perhaps the most important one. When it comes down to it, cigarette smoking and high blood pressure are usually indicators of something much larger: well-being (or, in this case, the lack thereof).

HAPPINESS AND THE BUBBLE

We also looked at the data about happiness levels in places hit hard by the housing crisis. Not surprisingly, we found that people in these places said they were much unhappier than people who lived in areas that were relatively unaffected.

From 2004 to 2010, the General Social Survey, a survey that monitors societal trends, asked a number of people a simple question: "Taken all together, how would you say things are these days—would you say that you are very happy, pretty happy, or not too happy?" The question may have been simple, but the answers turned out to be deeply revealing.

In 2004, only 9.9 percent of people in Texas and Tennessee labeled themselves "Not too happy." Six years later, in 2010, that number had only moved up by a few percentage points, to 13.1 percent. And that's not surprising, because Texas and Tennessee made it through the housing crisis relatively unscathed.

Compare that to places like Phoenix, Arizona, or the California metros of Bakersfield, Los Angeles, Riverside, Sacramento, and Vallejo. All of these metro areas were hit hard by the crash—and their survey data reflects that. The percentage of "not too happy" respondents clocked in at 16.5 percent in 2004, and then decreased as the housing bubble sent local home prices through the roof. In 2006, only 9.3 percent of these people were "not too happy." At the same time, a high of 33.2 percent of respondents actually said that they were *very* happy.

Sadly, the relative euphoria was short-lived. As the bubble burst, housing prices plummeted, and 20.2 percent of people in those markets told the General Social Survey that they weren't happy in 2010. As you might expect, the housing crisis made fully one out of every five people in these places "not too happy"—in other words, sad.

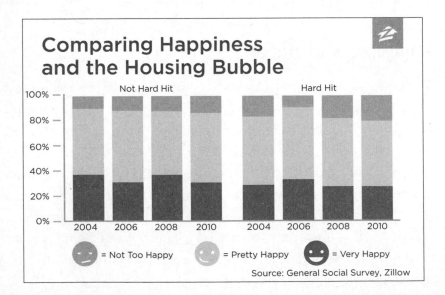

Comparing Happiness and the Housing Bubble

Source: General Social Survey, Zillow

Ultimately, it's easy to forget that behind the talk of booms and busts, mortgage rates and foreclosures, price hikes and drops, there are untold stories of stress headaches and cigarette smoking, marital strife and notices from the bank, and extra hours spent both at church and in traffic. Perhaps it's true that "statistics are people with the tears wiped off." At the same time, data also has the power to bring stories and struggles to life—and to help us deepen our understanding of the human experience...another reason the two of us wear the badge "numbers geek" with pride.

SEX, POLITICS, AND REAL ESTATE

There are two topics everyone knows not to bring up at a dinner party: politics and religion. Together with sex, these topics form a toxic trifecta that polite people simply don't bring up in polite company.

Luckily, these rules don't apply to books about real estate.

While we were getting to know the people behind the statistics, we started wondering how people's behaviors in these three unmentionable categories relate to whether they own or rent their homes. Are homeowners and renters voting for the same candidates? Who's going to church more? And, most importantly, who's having the most fun in the bedroom?

Using data from the General Social Survey, we decided to ask what would normally be considered rude questions and take a closer look at the relationship between renting, owning, and "the toxic trifecta."

Are renters all liberal heathens?

On the topic of politics, we found that homeowners tend to be more politically conservative overall than renters. (Which makes a certain amount of sense, given the emphasis conservatism places on property rights.) When asked whether they considered themselves politically liberal, moderate, or conservative, 40 percent of homeowners described themselves as "conservative," compared to only

25 percent of renters. When asked the same question, 34 percent of renters described themselves as "liberal," compared to only 24 percent of homeowners. This holds true for respondents both older and younger than forty-five.

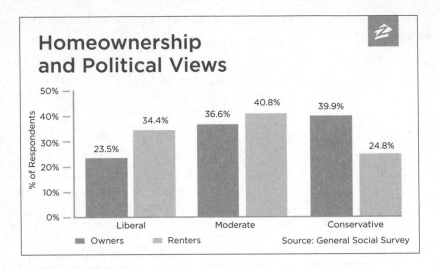

Homeowners also reported attending religious services more often than renters. Thirty-six percent of owners attend religious services weekly, compared to only 33 percent of renters. When we divided the respondents into two age groups and compared the younger group (aged forty-five or younger) to the older group (aged forty-six or older), we weren't surprised to see that the younger group attends religious services less frequently than the older group. But even within the younger group, younger owners are still attending services more often than younger renters. Nineteen percent of younger renters attend weekly services as compared to 32 percent of younger owners. Among the older group, the disparity is less drastic. Thirty-one percent of older renters attend weekly religious services, as compared to 39 percent of older owners. Maybe there's something about owning your own house—stronger ties to the community, for instance—that makes someone more likely to attend a house of worship.

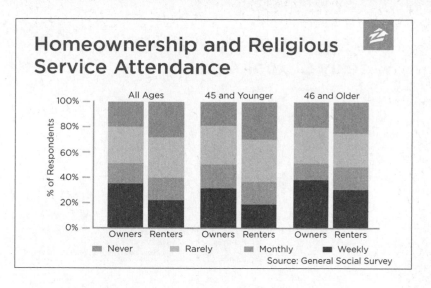

Homeownership and Religious Service Attendance

All Ages   45 and Younger   46 and Older

% of Respondents

100% —
80% —
60% —
40% —
20% —
0% —

Owners Renters   Owners Renters   Owners Renters

■ Never   ■ Rarely   ■ Monthly   ■ Weekly

Source: General Social Survey

Will buying a house improve your sex life?

Lastly, we took a peek into people's bedrooms, comparing homeownership to the data on frequency of sexual activity. A full 80 percent of both owners and renters reported being sexually active in the year before they were surveyed—but as it turns out, there's a lot more going on behind the doors of renters.

In every age group, the percentage of renters engaging in sexual activity at least once a week is greater or equal to the percentage of owners knocking boots. Nearly half—49 percent—of renters reported having sex at least once a week, as compared to 41 percent of owners. (This seems like a good point to reiterate that *correlation is not causation*. Tragically, going out and renting an apartment won't automatically make you more likely to see some action in it.)

For the youngest group (under thirty), 58 percent of renters reported weekly sexual activity, as compared to 54 percent of owners. In the next two age groups, the percentage of respondents not engaging in sexual activity was slightly smaller for owners, but renters were still having sex more often. For respondents aged thirty to forty-five, the weekly sexual scorecard is renters: 47 percent, owners: 42 percent. For the forty-six to fifty-nine group, that ratio

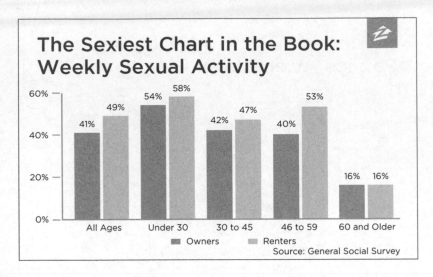

is 53 percent for renters, 40 percent for owners. And for people over sixty, fewer respondents, whether owners or renters, reported engaging in sexual activity in the previous year, though owners did come out ahead in this group. (The decline is probably due to the fact that more and more older adults—19 percent of men over sixty-five and 37 percent of women—are living alone.)

If this was a dinner party, everyone would probably have left the table in disgust by now, so we'll leave it there. But suffice it to say that, even when it comes to taboo topics, our homes can tell us a great deal about the most intimate parts of our lives.

Exterior of Flintstone family home from the TV show *The Flintstones (Courtesy of Everett Collection)*

23

What's Walkability Worth?

How Walkable Neighborhoods Affect Property Values

I (Spencer) love to walk. In fact, chances are, I'm taking a walk as you're reading this book. That is, taking a walk on my treadmill desk. I'm such a big fan of treadmill desks that we took a few conference rooms at Zillow HQ in Seattle and converted them into "walking rooms." Walking is a great way to stay healthy and energized—and I'm not the first one to take notice of that. "Walking," the ancient Greek physician Hippocrates observed, "is man's best medicine." Of course, man's second-best medicine in Hippocrates' day probably was leeches—and the good doctor had never seen an air-conditioned, self-parking Lexus with a seat-back TV screen to keep the kids entertained.

But we digress. There's no denying that people have liked to walk since well before the ancient Greeks. Fast-forward a couple of millennia, and walking is still all the rage, especially when it comes to real estate.

Ever since the 1980s, urban planners have tried to create diverse, sustainable, fully integrated—and walkable—communities. These are places where houses and workplaces are close to schools, parks, and shops, with trains and transit to transport people when walking becomes impractical. (Stan's doctoral dissertation in government from the University of Virginia focused on these "New

Urbanist" patterns; namely, whether greater economic scale—like big box stores and sprawl—had a negative impact on civic engagement. In case you're interested, it didn't.)

These planners use as their metric something called "the Popsicle test." In other words, they ask "Is this area sufficiently safe and navigable that an eight-year-old could walk or bike to the store and buy a Popsicle without needing to cross major highways, and return without it melting?"

Increasingly, developers are creating spaces that meet that standard—and people hipper than Hippocrates have flocked to them. "Walking to pick up milk, to nip over to the farmers' market, is priceless," one New Yorker told the *New York Times*. "It's more familiar, less suburban."[1] A Denver woman adds, "I just like being connected to everything down here—concerts, work, restaurants, all of it. This is where everything's at."[2]

Indeed, Millennials—people born after 1980—drive some 20 percent less than their parents did. They'd rather be on their smart phone than behind the wheel of a car. Aging Baby Boomers, too, are looking to drive less as they get older—or to "age in place" in a walkable neighborhood where they don't have to move when they no longer can drive.

And so, we became curious: If people are so attracted to areas where they can easily stroll to their office or a nice neighborhood bistro, what's walkability actually worth?

To answer that, we worked with our friends at Walk Score, who, coincidentally enough, are headquartered just a short walk from our offices in Seattle. In 2007, Jesse Kocher, Matt Lerner, and Mike Mathieu, along with CEO Josh Herst, created Walk Score to promote walkable, livable neighborhoods. During the years since, they have assigned a literal Walk Score®—on a 100-point scale—to every address in America, which measures how many amenities (restaurants, grocery stores, parks, schools, *etc.*) are located around a given home. And we followed their unique dataset to

some conclusions that are anything but pedestrian. Walk Scores®
are displayed on all homes' pages on Zillow.com.

The biggest takeaway is that home prices in more walkable areas
offer higher returns and recover faster from market downturns.

Our second insight is that what walkability is worth really
depends on you. If you value living in a walkable area, then a
higher Walk Score® means higher home prices. If you're fine driving instead, a higher Walk Score® can actually mean *lower* home
prices.

Let's walk through those conclusions.

WALKABLE MEANS WEALTH

Major American metros offer a wide variety of walking experiences—
from the Brooklynites traipsing easily between brownstone and
farmers' market, to the Phoenix residents driving a half-mile to get
to the movies. To capture this variation, we sliced, diced, and analyzed Walk Score's data by their four categories of walkability: "car
dependent," "somewhat walkable," "very walkable," and "walker's
paradise."

On one extreme are cities like Washington, DC, with nearly 45
percent of the city considered at least Somewhat Walkable and over
6.5 percent classified as a "walker's paradise"—meaning you could
walk to work, pick up a nice rotisserie chicken on the way home,
and take your kid to the park all without ever getting into a car. On
the opposite end of the spectrum are Las Vegas and Riverside, at 86
and 91 percent "car dependent," respectively.

When we analyze the median home values within each of these
categories across major American metros, we see several clear
trends.

First, more walkable areas offer higher returns. Since 2000,
median home values in "very walkable" and "walker's paradise"
neighborhoods have appreciated more than their counterparts in

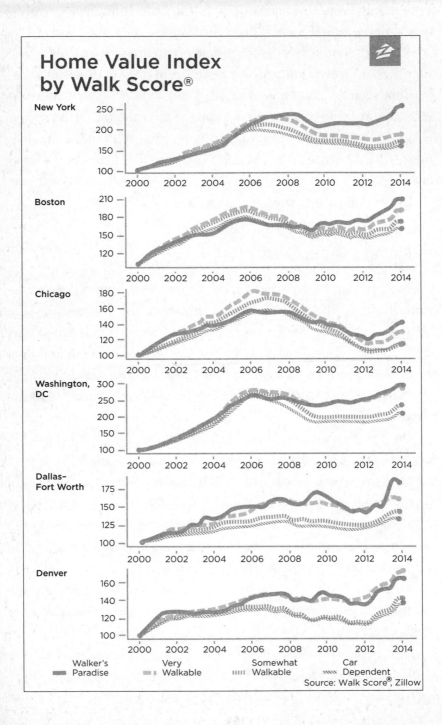

Home Value Index by Walk Score®

New York

Boston

Chicago

Washington, DC

Dallas–Fort Worth

Denver

Walker's Paradise | Very Walkable | Somewhat Walkable | Car Dependent

Source: Walk Score®, Zillow

less walkable locations. In Chicago and New York, homes in walkable places appreciated 162 percent and 161 percent, respectively, faster than homes in "car dependent" areas. In Dallas-Fort Worth and Denver, where the housing crisis was milder, "walker's paradise" homes are now worth more than 1.75 times and 1.65 times what they were a decade and a half earlier, respectively. Conversely, in these same cities, "car dependent" homes are worth only 1.3 and 1.4 times as much, respectively.

Second, more walkable areas are more resilient. We found that, on average, walkable areas recovered faster from the Great Recession. In DC and Boston, for instance, "very walkable" and "walker's paradise" home values hardly dropped relative to "somewhat walkable" and "car dependent" home prices. In fact, they now surpass peak levels.

WHAT WALKABILITY IS WORTH DEPENDS ON YOU

So the data suggests that Walk Score® is a strong signal to home buyers that more walkable areas are of higher value. But that still doesn't tell us whether access to walkable amenities is actually what people are paying for.

After all, higher home values could instead reflect all the other things that come with walkable areas—things like proximity to big city entertainment or income levels. Using something called "log-linear hedonic regressions," we controlled for all those other variables and came to the classic economist's answer: *It depends.*

Finding a home is all about trade-offs, so ask yourself this question: Do you really love walking? Do you agree with the twentieth-century English writer Cyril Connolly that "No city should be too large for a man to walk out of in a morning?" Is walkability a home feature on which you refuse to compromise? If so, then read on.

If you choose to live in a walkable neighborhood, then you're likely someone who places a premium on a higher Walk Score®.

And you aren't alone. In these neighborhoods, the higher the Walk Score®, the higher the home price.

In a city like Chicago—where Walk Score® has the biggest impact on home values—we found that fifteen points of greater walkability can mean *nearly a 25 percent* increase in home price.

The Effect of Walk Score®

Metro Area	Effect of 15 More Walk Score® Points (% of home price)	Implied Cost ($)	A homeowner can accept the following and a Very Walkable home OR a home in a Walker's Paradise for the same amount of money			Change in Commute Time (minutes)
			Bigger Home (square feet)	More Bathrooms	Higher Neighborhood Income ($)	
Chicago, IL	24	55,571	2,537	0.9	27,414	-18.9
Miami–Ft. Lauderdale, FL	21	41,475	322	1.5	33,871	16.4
Pittsburgh, PA	21	28,749	436	1.1	15,110	-12.1
Dallas–Ft. Worth, TX	20	37,786	359	1.6	32,951	-7.7
Tampa, FL	19	29,606	311	1.1	9,057	-6.3
Washington, DC	18	71,033	474	1.4	—	-10.6
Los Angeles, CA	18	87,120	332	1.9	22,975	-5
Detroit, MI	18	30,345	497	0.6	13,125	-6.2
St. Louis, MO	18	31,576	464	1.3	16,840	-1
Philadelphia, PA	16	35,864	1,289	0.4	11,642	-4.7
Boston, MA	13	46,725	346	0.6	30,341	-49.4
Baltimore, MD	12	35,483	281	1	—	-3.8
Cincinnati, OH	12	18,000	263	1	4,781	—
Atlanta, GA	11	20,250	203	0.9	13,554	-3.3
San Diego, CA	10	42,413	225	0.6	12,500	-1.3
San Francisco, CA	10	57,330	195	0.9	16,525	-5.6
Seattle, WA	9	31,155	207	1.7	30,000	-5.3
Cleveland, OH	9	12,261	147	0.7	7,439	-5.8
Sacramento, CA	9	24,780	174	0.9	6,189	-0.6
Portland, OR	8	21,457	201	1	18,000	-10.8
Phoenix, AZ	8	15,444	120	—	6,555	-4.1
Riverside, CA	7	20,273	159	—	9,684	—
Denver, CO	6	15,621	169	0.5	9,318	-0.9
Minneapolis–St. Paul, MN	4	8,708	86	0.5	5,000	-1.9
New York, NY	4	14,184	3,000	0.1	17,143	2.7

That translates to paying over $55,000 more on a $233,000 house—just to live in, say, The Loop instead of Avondale.

There are a lot of ways to think about that trade-off. You might choose to live in a slightly less walkable area of Chicago, but that would give you a home with 2,537 more square feet, or another bathroom, or even a commute that's nearly twenty minutes shorter. Or you could keep the extra cash you'd save from living in a less walkable area and use it for a new car, to make driving more enjoyable.

Of course, not everyone sees walkability as the one indispensable feature of a home. Many of us are OK living in "car dependent" areas. And for these would-be homeowners—in areas that are not classified as at least "somewhat walkable"—we discovered that higher Walk Scores® actually translate to *lower* home values. Put another way, a higher Walk Score® only improves home values if your community is classified as "somewhat walkable," "very walkable," or a "walker's paradise."

For example, in Cleveland and Baltimore's "car dependent" neighborhoods, homes in those areas that are 15 points more walkable actually yield 8.25 percent and 8.4 percent *less* in home value, respectively—a far cry from Chicago's 24 percent premium. In Baltimore, that's an implied drop in home value of nearly $24,000.

Is this somewhat counterintuitive? You bet.

But think about it this way: People in "car dependent" areas may value different local amenities—for instance, they may care more about award-winning schools nearby than a James Beard Award–winning chef at the local tapas bar.

Or, since Walk Score® doesn't say anything about the quality of the amenities in the vicinity, the cause could be what we call our Strip-Mall Hypothesis. In other words, there may be shopping and dining options in the more walkable clusters of car dependent areas, but they might be of the strip-mall variety—necessary, but preferably not within walking distance for an eight-year-old with a melting Popsicle.

WALKING OFF INTO THE SUNSET

The bottom line is that the desire to be walking distance from the friends and amenities that make up our daily lives isn't going away anytime soon. This is not just another *New York Times* trend piece about the habits of young people sporting plaid and eating only locally sourced food.

Between planes, trains, and automobiles, we may have more ways than ever to get around in the twenty-first century, but a lot of us still seem to agree with Hippocrates on the virtues of walking. And that means an even bigger push among planners and builders to continue creating walkable spaces.

Home values reflect the fact that these more walkable areas can offer huge financial returns. Yet the decision about where you want to live (and on what you're willing to compromise) is an utterly personal one, as we've discussed throughout this book. *Walkability definitely matters*. It has real, lasting impact on the dollars and cents in your bank account. But the *difference* in value corresponds to *what* you value.

THIS OLD HOUSING MARKET

RETHINKING REAL ESTATE IN AMERICA

Exterior of the plantation Tara, from the movie *Gone with the Wind* (MGM/ *Photofest*)

Owning Isn't for Everyone

The Case for Decoupling Homeownership and the American Dream

On a balmy day in June 2002, President George W. Bush visited Atlanta, Georgia, to promote his administration's efforts to dramatically increase homeownership rates among low-income Americans, and particularly among minorities. Bush pointed out that while 75 percent of white Americans owned their own homes, the homeownership rate among African Americans and Hispanics was less than 50 percent. "And that has got to change for the good of the country," he said.[1]

To narrow this alarming gap, Bush announced a series of efforts that he claimed would help 5.5 million low-income and minority families purchase their own homes by the end of the decade. The biggest barrier to homeownership for these families, Bush noted, was that many simply didn't have enough cash on hand for the 10 or 20 percent down payment required to secure a mortgage. So he called on Congress to create a $200 million "American Dream Down Payment Fund" to provide up to $10,000 per eligible family to cover down-payment and closing costs. Bush also highlighted the shortage of affordable housing units for sale. To fix that problem, Bush asked Congress to pass $2.4 billion in new tax cuts for developers to build low-cost units in struggling neighborhoods.

Wealth redistribution? Massive government spending? Investing billions of dollars in low-income neighborhoods? The federal government meddling with the real estate market? If a time machine suddenly plopped you down at the president's announcement, you couldn't be blamed for thinking the speaker was Barack Obama wearing a "W" mask. For a fiercely conservative Republican, the programs Bush announced were extraordinarily, and confusingly, progressive.

But that's the amazing thing about housing. It is, and always has been, a largely nonpartisan issue in America. Our Founding Fathers— Federalists and Republicans, alike—revered homeownership, equating it with freedom, independence, and civic republican virtue. In the early 1800s, Thomas Jefferson wrote that the average citizen's right to property was "the true foundation of republican government."

As the nation expanded, the United States government redistributed so-called "unassigned" (i.e., confiscated from Native Americans) lands—literally for free—to settlers who agreed to "improve" or build and maintain homes on them.

During the 1930s, Franklin D. Roosevelt, whose alphabet soup of New Deal agencies enabled home loans for tens of millions of Americans, proclaimed that a nation of homeowners was "unconquerable"; his GI Bill turned millions of returning servicemen into homeowners almost overnight by offering generous loan guarantees.[2]

In 1992, Congress sought to expand homeownership opportunities by mandating that Fannie Mae and Freddie Mac, the entities that help provide mortgages to most Americans, make a larger share of their mortgages available to low-income and minority applicants. Initially, this share was pegged at 30 percent. Later it increased to more than half of all their mortgages. This dramatic expansion was designed to boost overall homeownership, and in 1994, Bill Clinton set an explicit target of raising the homeownership rate in America from the historical average of 64 percent to the (then) unprecedented rate of 67.5 percent by 2000. Clinton declared at the time, "When we boost the number of homeowners...we strengthen our economy, create jobs, build up the middle class, and build better citizens."[3]

It's no surprise, then, that George W. Bush would follow in the footsteps of his presidential predecessors by attempting to expand the circle of homeownership to include low-income families—and, in doing so, to give a shot in the arm to downtrodden neighborhoods across the nation. Back in 2003, this seemed like a really great idea, and everyone was on board. In fact, Congress passed the American Dream Down Payment Act *unanimously*. That's right: Homeownership was (and still is) such a popular and powerful idea that every single Republican and Democrat in Congress got behind "W"'s bill.

As an aside, you may be surprised to learn that while we may lead the world in pro-homeowner rhetoric, we're significant laggards when it comes to actual homeownership. During the previous

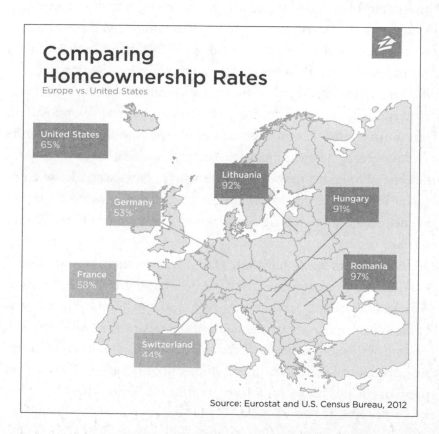

Comparing Homeownership Rates
Europe vs. United States

United States
65%

Lithuania
92%

Germany
53%

Hungary
91%

France
58%

Romania
97%

Switzerland
44%

Source: Eurostat and U.S. Census Bureau, 2012

three decades, the US homeownership rate has hovered around 65 percent, far behind the rates of many other countries.

Nevertheless, the bipartisan bubble, like the housing bubble, was destined to pop. And when it did, so did the global economy. A lot of the folks President Bush was trying to help ended up in dire straits, and many of the neighborhoods he hoped to rejuvenate became foreclosure wastelands.

Just consider what happened to Darrin West. Darrin was an Atlanta police officer who attended President Bush's speech that day in 2002. He wasn't there to protect the president, though. He was there as the president's guest.

Darrin had recently purchased his own home in Park Place South, a new mixed-use residential community that the Atlanta Development Authority was building in what had been (until they bought the land and bulldozed the existing, crumbling homes) a run-down neighborhood.[4] Darrin was one of the first homeowners in the new development, and he purchased his $130,000 town house with a $20,000 loan from the City of Atlanta to cover his down payment.

Bush announced his low-income and minority homeownership program at a church near the Park Place South development. In fact, Bush toured Darrin's home before the announcement. During his speech, he even cited Darrin and his neighbors as exactly the type of folks his new homeownership policies were designed to help. "What we've got to do," Bush said, "is to figure out how to make sure these stories are repeated over and over and over again in America."[5]

In the years that followed, Darrin's story *was* repeated over and over again. Across the United States, hundreds of thousands of Americans just like Darrin bought a home for the first time. It was a time of real estate excitement and heady optimism that didn't last for long. When the *New York Times* tracked Darrin down in 2008, the paper discovered that, like millions of Americans, Darrin and many of his neighbors no longer lived in or owned their homes—the bank did.[6]

Perhaps the worst part of this story is that it could have been avoided, for Darrin and many other low-income homeowners, if only the president and policy makers in Washington had a better grasp of the data.

Based on our analysis of home values during the past two decades, one thing is crystal clear: Subsidies for low-income families to buy homes in low-income neighborhoods ultimately hurt the very people they purport to help. And the problem with this policy isn't just that it fails in its goals of creating wealth and opportunity; it's that it can actually destroy them.

There are a number of reasons behind this, but they boil down to a simple fact: *Buying a home is a gamble.* It's a gamble that we will want to keep living in one place—and keep making the mortgage payments that come with it—for years and even decades into the future. The problem is that people who live paycheck to paycheck sometimes can't afford that gamble. Instead of locking themselves into a mortgage, they are sometimes better off having the flexibility to adapt their lives to changes they might face in the future.

Let's say, for instance, that you have a steady job in Cleveland, so you buy a home not far from work. If the economy turns sour and you lose that job, you're suddenly tied to a city where you don't have an income. You can look for a new job in Cleveland, of course, but it might also make sense to move to a nearby city that offers more work. This kind of job mobility is especially important to people with smaller savings accounts, who can't afford too much time without a paycheck coming in. But if they're tied down with a home and a mortgage, that kind of strategic move is much more difficult to make.

If you own a home, it also can be much harder to deal with other catastrophic events. Maybe one of your children gets sick and you wind up footing a ten-thousand-dollar hospital bill. At a moment of crisis like that, it might make sense to reduce some of your expenses. This may be easy enough if you rent your home, because you can always move into a cheaper place. But if you own a house, you're pretty much stuck with that monthly mortgage payment—and a big, unexpected expense can wreak havoc on your budget.

It can be even more disastrous for a low-income person if declining home values cause their home to sink into negative equity. Every time a homeowner writes a check to pay off a home that's worth less than they bought it for, their financial security takes a serious hit. For people without much financial security in the first place, that blow can be devastating. They wind up trapped in these homes, unable to sell, watching their savings and their paychecks dwindle away every month. Homes that were supposed to secure their financial futures destroy them instead.

Moreover, many of these low-income home purchases are bad investments, whether or not they ultimately plunge the owners underwater. Our analysis shows that even if the housing market hadn't crashed, pushing homeownership on everyone, everywhere would *still* have had harmful effects on those buyers' pocketbooks.

Why? Because, it turns out, the extent to which a house gains or loses value widely correlates with the affluence of the neighborhood in which it's located.

In other words, for more affluent areas, housing returns tend to be higher and more stable. In less affluent areas, housing returns tend to be lower and more volatile. As Thomas Thibodeau, a professor at the University of Colorado's Leeds School of Business and a Zillow technical advisor, argues in his research that inspired our own, encouraging low-income families to invest in under-performing communities doesn't free these families from the cycle of poverty—it *further traps them in it.*

To illustrate the point, let's take a look at our country's second- and third-biggest metropolitan areas, Los Angeles and Chicago. These sprawling metros have dozens of neighborhoods, which gives us a big sample of communities to analyze. By cross-referencing Census data with the Zillow Home Value Index, we can see how home values have fared in poorer and wealthier areas over time.

In Los Angeles, during the past seventeen years, only three ZIP codes have seen their homes' values depreciate by 3 percentage points or more annually. All three are poorer neighborhoods, according to Census data. Meanwhile, during the same time frame, the twenty-three ZIP codes that represent the most affluent communities in LA had an average return of 6.5 percent per year. Home values fell the most in Hawaiian Gardens, a neighborhood where the average annual income is $42,770. And prices rose the fastest in Newport Beach, where the average household earns $101,324 a year.

This pattern holds true in the Windy City as well. Since 1996, looking at all the neighborhoods in Chicago where home values depreciated the most, the vast majority of them (80 percent) were poorer, on average, than the rest of the metro area. On the other hand, *all* of the Chicago neighborhoods in which home values appreciated the most were wealthier than the city at large.

When it comes to homeownership across the nation, these examples show one way in which the rich are getting richer, and the poor are getting poorer. Although less affluent areas across the United States don't necessarily see home values nose-diving as in the cases above, it is a fairly persistent pattern that more affluent areas see much higher returns, and less affluent areas see far lower returns.

The disparity in performance is especially startling. Richer neighborhoods see 60 percent higher returns, on average, than poorer neighborhoods. The result of this dynamic is not only that the affluent get more affluent, but that they become so *faster*. Their investment appreciates quicker than the real estate investments of less affluent homeowners in less affluent neighborhoods.

What's more, our analysis shows that home values are much more volatile at the lower end of the housing spectrum. As the affluence of a neighborhood increases, the risks associated with housing prices decrease. Therefore, the data tells us, housing is an inherently riskier and underperforming investment in less affluent areas. In essence, buyers in poorer neighborhoods are making investments with both lower rates of return and higher volatility—a dangerous combination that we see virtually nowhere else in the economy.

(The only instance in which this isn't the case is in extremely wealthy neighborhoods, where home prices tend to be just as volatile as in economically depressed communities. Of course, if you're well-to-do, and you buy a pricey house that depreciates, chances are you can take the hit if you sell for less than you bought. If you're a low-income family, however, it's likely that you can't cover the loss, and the only option is to default on your mortgage.)

Which brings us back to Park Place South. When President Bush visited Atlanta, he told his audience that homeownership is part and parcel of the American Dream. "I believe those of us who have been given positions of responsibility must do everything we can to spotlight the dream and to make sure the dream shines in all neighborhoods, all throughout our country," he said. "Right here in America if you own your own home, you're realizing the American Dream."

The sentiment is beautiful, and no doubt, Bush was heartfelt in speaking those words. It's also an idea many of us share, because it's deeply embedded in our nation's laws, values, and cultural norms. We unquestioningly assume that homeownership equals better citizenship, in spite of the fact that the research suggests otherwise.

The connection between housing and the American Dream is so strong that it seems scandalous to even consider, empirically speaking, whether homeownership makes sense for all low-income Americans. And the mythology of the American Dream is only part of the reason why. It's a very intuitive idea that helping people buy their own homes is a great way to grow wealth and lessen the divide between the haves and the have-nots.

Unfortunately, as unsettling as it may be, the very opposite is true.

Please don't shoot the messenger, here. This isn't our opinion; it's our conclusion based on the data. And the data doesn't lie. Equating homeownership with the American Dream is simply, and indisputably, a policy nightmare.

This conclusion, needless to say, is incredibly disturbing. We all know about the rising income and wealth disparity in America.

It's been an ongoing trend for decades, and most everyone loathes it. At a fundamental level—at a moral level, even—this inequality is deeply upsetting. And, according to economists, there's good reason for us to feel that way. The latest research shows that rising inequality actually hurts overall economic growth and suppresses GDP.[7] So it's a very positive thing that our people, and our presidents, want the country to be more equal, not less.

But we need to focus on policies that truly lead to prosperity, not just assume that homeownership will lead to it. Trying to engineer prosperity through homeownership might *feel* like the right thing to do.

As we've shown, however, it is a terrible idea. Perversely, the policies that attempt to decrease inequality by increasing homeownership will just end up exacerbating the problem we all want to address. They help low-income families to buy properties that are risky and that underperform over time relative to the rest of the nation's housing stock. At the end of the day, there's a real chance that a mortgage on a risky home will decrease a low-income family's chance of achieving and living the American Dream.

Fortunately, plenty of other policies have been proven to lift the economic prospects of low-income and minority Americans, like no-interest student loans, free or heavily discounted in-state college tuition, and expanding the Earned Income Tax Credit, which puts more cash in workers' pockets each year to spend, save, or invest as they see fit. There are also successful affordable housing policies, such as the Low Income Housing Tax Credit, which encourages private investment in building affordable housing units. And it goes without saying that these policies don't come with the unfortunate, occasional side effect of creating economy-destroying bubbles in the marketplace.

Homes—and the very idea of homeownership—evoke a strong emotional reaction in all of us. Even in our presidents. In all things housing, it's important to listen to our instincts, but it's better to trust the data.

Exterior of the Cohen family home from the TV show *The OC (Photofest)*

The Third Rail of Real Estate

Is the Mortgage Interest Deduction Really the Best Use of $100 Billion?

If there's one thing on which Americans of all stripes seem to agree, it's the indisputable importance of a section buried deep within the 75,000-page federal tax code that allows homeowners to deduct the interest on their mortgages. In 2011, for instance, a New York Times/CBS poll found that more than *90 percent* of Americans— Californians and Texans, Red Sox and Yankees fans, Android devotees and iPhone zealots—believed it was important to continue the deduction. Even during the 2012 presidential campaign, when Barack Obama and Mitt Romney could hardly concur on the color of the sky, both candidates voiced support for the Mortgage Interest Deduction, or, in real-estate parlance, the MID.

As it turns out, the MID is an accident, a historical fluke, a vestige from a bygone era that still casts a multi-billion-dollar shadow. The legislators who first enacted the MID would probably be surprised to see the proportions the deduction has taken on—both in its popularity with the American people and in the hefty $100 billion it costs Uncle Sam in tax revenue every year. And, similarly, most Americans would probably be surprised to hear how this deduction came to exist at all.

Back in 1913, Congress wrote the first ever federal income tax bill, after securing a constitutional amendment just to propose it.

The country's mood was cautious, and Congress hardly wanted to overreach. Lawmakers decided to give the public as little to oppose as possible by imposing only a 1 percent tax on incomes over $3,000—leaving more than 99 percent of Americans untouched. What's more, in calculating taxable income, Congress agreed to deduct *all* consumer interest—including mortgage interest—from gross income, chalking it up to the cost of doing business (it literally was "business," since essentially all debt back then came from running a business). At that time, fewer than half of Americans even owned homes, and only about a third of them on credit. So it wasn't as if Congress had deliberately singled out homeownership as something especially worthy of a deduction. If anything, the deduction was more like a historical accident.

The write-off for consumer interest might have continued on in obscurity, but after World War II, the amount of consumer credit began to balloon as more and more Americans started buying goods and financing part of the cost. The skyrocketing amount of mortgage debt was fueled by returning GIs looking to settle down, new home-building technology, and new financing options for home buying. Auto-loan, credit-card, and student debt skyrocketed as well. As a result of this credit boom, when President Reagan initiated substantial tax reform in 1986—the first major overhaul of the US tax system since 1954—the US Department of the Treasury recommended that *all* of these consumer interest deductions, such as credit-card debt, be eliminated. That's right: At the time, you could actually deduct your unpaid credit-card balance. And sure enough, one by one, these deductions were axed—except for the MID.

Reagan earlier had declared, "the taxing power of government... must not be used to regulate the economy or bring about social change." But thanks to a major lobbying effort by the National Association of Realtors, he decided to make one exception—the boosting of homeownership. In their definitive account of the historic 1986 Tax Reform Act, *Showdown at Gucci Gulch*, reporters Jeffrey H. Birnbaum and Alan S. Murray wrote that even in the midst of the most sweeping tax reform effort in a century, "the mere thought of tampering with [the mortgage interest deduction] was unpatriotic." Reagan promised, "We will preserve the part of the American dream which the home-mortgage-interest deduction symbolizes." The MID, he told Congress, was "off the table."

And off the table it has remained, immune to ideology, untroubled by the coming and going of successive presidents and Congresses. After a century, the MID has gone, as University of California, Davis Professor Dennis J. Ventry Jr. put it, "from accident to birthright, from one of many deductible personal interest items to one of the few still standing, and from a negligible tax offset to the second most expensive tax subsidy."[1] It has found a home in the tax code—and it's an awfully cozy one. In 2013, the federal government paid about $55 billion for both veteran's health care[2] and foreign aid.[3] It spent about $82 billion on food stamps.[4] And yet the MID trumped these national priorities, keeping $100 billion out of the United States Treasury.[5]

Today, fiscal austerity is all the rage, tax reform is a perennially hot topic of conversation in Washington, and all tax deductions— even the coziest ones—are candidates for the chopping block. Still, there's a general reluctance to even consider getting rid of the MID, and considerable fear about what would happen to the housing market if it were to vanish. The flamboyant financier and real estate magnate Donald Trump voiced the concerns of many Americans (and some self-serving real estate developers) when he blustered that doing away with the MID would be a "total catastrophe," leading "to a major recession, if not a depression."

He's not the only member of the real estate community to voice this concern. The National Association of Realtors has said that the MID "is vital to the health and stability of housing markets." Any change to this policy, they argue, could "marginalize current and future home buyers as well as jeopardize the nascent housing recovery and the overall economy."[6]

This is the prevailing view in the world of real estate professionals.

In a recent Zillow survey of more than 1,200 real estate agents, most agents surveyed (68 percent) believed that the MID should remain intact with no changes.

But we don't think real estate agents should be quite so fearful about losing the MID—and most economists agree with us. When we compared the survey of real estate agents to the Zillow Home Price Expectations Survey of 113 leading housing economists, real estate agents were much more pessimistic about removing the mortgage interest deduction than economists. In fact, *half* of the economists said they would phase out or eliminate the deduction as soon as possible—and another quarter would restrict MID eligibility.

Moreover, there's a real-world example that should put MID defenders' minds at ease. Many argue that the MID encourages homeownership and builds strong communities. But we don't have to look far to find a place without this deduction that still has extremely high homeownership—nearly 70 percent—and cities listed among the world's most livable. It's a nation with flourishing neighborhood associations and robust civic participation. More than half the country considers itself part of the growing middle class; their kids go to good neighborhood schools and play in well-manicured yards.

This country is Canada. And Canadians built all of this without a mortgage interest deduction. In fact, they have almost the exact same homeownership rate as the United States.[7] And given their experience just across our northern border, it's hard to argue that the MID is essential to keeping our real estate market strong.

Granted, if US lawmakers eliminate the MID, home prices might take a slight hit. But our analysis shows that while some existing homeowners would experience decreases in home values, many more potential buyers would gain in terms of home affordability. Remember, there are two sides to this equation: buyers and sellers. Even if a slight decrease in home values wouldn't be the best news for sellers, it *would* be great news for buyers. And our housing market would still be going strong.

In general, economists also believe that the minor dip in home prices would be much less cataclysmic than real estate agents fear. Indeed, most of the decrease in home values would likely be confined to high-end homes in affluent areas, which have seen robust recovery, and generally outperform less affluent markets. As the Urban Institute succinctly notes, "the best available evidence predicts far less dire effects and suggests that some reforms to the MID could actually bolster the housing market recovery."[8]

To understand why this would be, the first thing to note is that most Americans won't be affected at all if the MID disappears. That's because the MID is a *deduction*, which means it's relevant only to people who (a) pay federal income taxes, and (b) itemize their deductions. As Mitt Romney (to his chagrin) reminded the world during the 2012 presidential campaign, 47 percent of Americans don't pay federal income tax (in 2013, it was actually 46 percent). This is not because they're cheating the federal government, though. Most of the folks who don't pay federal income taxes are low-income workers, unemployed, or retired. Of the 53 percent of Americans who *do* pay federal income taxes, only about one-third itemize their deductions. That means right off the bat, the MID is irrelevant to all but about one in six Americans. And if you subtract the 20 percent[9] of itemizers who rent or have paid off their homes, the pool of potential beneficiaries is even smaller. All told, only about two in every fifteen Americans, roughly 13 percent, take the mortgage interest deduction every year.

Nevertheless, even though the MID affects fewer than one-eighth of all Americans, we're still talking about millions of families. Won't they suffer if the mortgage interest deduction goes away? Well, yes, they might. But it turns out that even then, the effects are fairly localized. We analyzed what would happen to homeowners if the federal government were to cap itemized deductions at $25,000 per household. This could be a real possibility, given that politicians of both major political parties have proposed plans along these lines. But even if this comes to pass, the effects would be nearly all on the coasts, with vast swaths of the country completely untouched.

Moreover, within those clusters of areas affected, we found some fairly telling facts. Of the top one hundred ZIP codes likely to be hardest-hit, the mean home value is—are you ready for this?—$865,241. In other words, the federal government is spending $100 billion every year to help Americans who live in almost million-dollar homes! This is the very definition of a regressive policy—one that focuses virtually all of its benefits on the people who are already the most well off. Given that, it's especially ironic that the MID is consistently sold to the American people as a populist policy designed to help the little guy. In reality, it's the exact opposite. Generally speaking, only the well-to-do would feel the pinch if the MID were to be eliminated.

In 2003, two professors at the University of Pennsylvania's Wharton School of Business calculated that the MID amounts to a subsidy of up to $26,385 for the limited number of home buyers who qualify.[10] That's half the median household income in the United States[11] going to help homeowners who make well more than that. A Reason Foundation report found that nearly 75 percent of tax filers claiming the MID had incomes over $200,000, for an average tax savings of $2,221. The remaining 25 percent who filed taxes and took advantage of the MID saved less than $114 on average.[12] It is, as one economist calls it, "the quintessential 'upside-down subsidy': the greater the need, the smaller the subsidy."

That's already a curious public policy decision. But it gets worse.

For one thing, these subsidies don't just support wealthy homeowners' lavish tastes; they make them *more* lavish. According to our analysis, in those same ZIP codes, the average square footage per house is 27 percent *larger* than in the surrounding metro counties. We don't just subsidize luxury with the $100 billion we set aside for the MID; *we purchase sprawl.*

Well, we certainly don't want government to subsidize big homes and bad spending habits for the wealthiest Americans. But, you might be wondering, what about middle-class homeowners? Don't they benefit from the MID? Isn't there anyone who truly uses the deduction to make the leap from tenant to homeowner?

According to our analysis, a sizeable portion of the one hundred most-affected ZIP codes *do* have median household incomes of $75,000 or less, but nearly all of them are located in and around the New York metro area—an extremely expensive region with many renters. While we would certainly feel for these less affluent home-owners if the MID were to be phased out—and would welcome a deduction that better targeted them—we find it disconcerting that one of the largest deductions in the federal tax code benefits such a small sliver of citizens.

So, you may be asking, with *what*, exactly, might our policy makers *replace* the MID? How can government be a help to home buyers without also being a hindrance to taxpayers?

Well, we believe that the best solutions correspond with the actual problems.

For many first-time buyers, the biggest hurdle to homeowner-ship is the down payment. Therefore, the vast majority of Ameri-cans would be far better off if Washington scrapped the MID for a refundable, first-time home buyer tax credit, or even a first-time home buyer cash grant. This kind of progressive policy—which aids less affluent buyers more than it does wealthier ones—would make a huge difference in many peoples' lives. Moreover, this one-time benefit wouldn't blow such a big hole in the federal budget because Washington wouldn't be subsidizing the same, relatively few well-to-do homeowners over and over, year after year.

Another way to look at the MID is this: For $230,000, you can buy a brand-new condo in Colorado Springs, or a brand-new Ferrari 458 Italia. Why does the federal government let you deduct your interest payment on one but not the other? Looking at the data, we believe the billions Washington spends on the MID could really be better directed.

Exterior of the character Sam Baldwin's houseboat home in the movie *Sleepless in Seattle (Photofest)*

Down by the Seaside

*How Waterfront Property Plays by
Its Own Rules*

As the winds swept through downtown New Orleans, they gusted to upward of 125 miles per hour. They already had smashed through Grand Isle, Louisiana, and destroyed whole parishes. The river rose ten feet over the Big Easy, tearing ships and tugs from their moorings. Hundreds of barges sank or were driven aground. Raging water swept through entire neighborhoods, leveling everything in sight. The storm surge collapsed into Lake Pontchartrain, just north of New Orleans, and the Mississippi River Gulf Outlet to the east and the south. Overwhelmed by the powerful crush of water, the surrounding levees failed, unleashing devastating floods that submerged the city, including the low-lying Ninth Ward, leaving much of it underwater for days. All told, 164,000 homes were flooded. New Orleans was destroyed.

No, this wasn't Hurricane Katrina in 2005.

This was Hurricane Betsy in 1965.

Forty years before the name "Katrina" was forever sullied by the deadliest storm in US history, a category 3 hurricane pummeled much of the Gulf Coast in what became America's first billion-dollar disaster. And during the years since, nearly every time a coastal disaster strikes, history repeats. Levees and other protections fail. Homes are damaged and destroyed. Inadequate insurance leaves people out to dry. The government spends billions rescuing whole communities—the right, but expensive, thing to do.

Why do people keep building their homes and lives in places that are so prone to becoming disaster zones? And why does the government keep backstopping waterfront real estate?

We turned to the data to find out, and one fact became immediately clear: Coastal real estate operates according to its very own, unique rules—rules that help us understand the costly cycle of creation and destruction, and perhaps can help us learn how to break it.

ON THE WATERFRONT

Terrifying stories of loss of property, and occasionally loss of life, should be enough to send prospective home buyers scrambling inland to higher, safer ground. And yet, despite the grave (and growing) risks of living beachside, our analysis shows that coastal housing markets are virtually guaranteed to succeed. People simply want to live on or near the water—no matter what.

This may sound obvious, but from an economic standpoint, it's a little bizarre. After all, if we've learned anything during the *past* decade, it's that extreme weather events like devastating hurricanes are only going to increase in the *coming* decades. As the National Climate Assessment recently affirmed, "human induced climate change is projected to continue and accelerate significantly if emissions of heat trapping gases continue to increase."[1]

As much as we'd love to see electric cars and solar panels dramatically cut the world's carbon emissions, it doesn't seem likely to happen anytime soon. Much to our chagrin, it's probably the case that global climate change will continue unabated, seas will rise, and severe weather events will become more frequent. As a result, communities around the country will be faced with even more devastating floods caused by storm surges.

Coastal living has always been risky, but it's becoming even riskier than ever before. But that current and future risk just isn't reflected in the cost of coastal real estate. In fact, no matter how severe the risk, we found that buyers will always pay a premium for properties near and on the water.

Consider our analysis of ZIP codes within twenty miles of the coast in Florida, North Carolina, and South Carolina—three states that are routinely devastated by tropical storms. We divided the ZIP codes in these states into three groups: those that are on the coast, within 10 miles of the coast, and within 20 miles of the coast. We then calculated the median home value for each group by state each and every month from July 1997 to November 2012—a period of time during which coastal storms were particularly frequent and destructive.

Given the choice between living within 10 miles of the coast or right on it, we found that buyers will pay 58 percent more in Florida, 38 percent more in North Carolina, and 22 percent more in South Carolina to live in homes on oceanfront property—despite the inherent risk to these homes given their proximity to the water and vulnerability to flooding.

The trend continues farther inland. Want to live within 10 miles off the coast? Median property values in Florida, North Carolina, and South Carolina are 5 percent, 7 percent, and 17 percent higher, respectively, than those located between 10 and 20 miles from the coast.

The most remarkable feature of this trend, however, is that it seems to go unchanged even in the *aftermath* of major storms.

The graph on the next page plots the median home values for coastal properties in Florida. Out of the seven hurricanes noted on the graph—Floyd, Irene (1999), Charley, Frances, Jeanne, Katrina, and Wilma—Irene alone caused approximately $600 million of flood damage.[2] Nevertheless, our analysis shows no discernible dips in the median value of coastal homes in the wake of these severe storms.

Given how invincible waterfront property values seem to be, it's no wonder that coastal properties also weathered the bursting

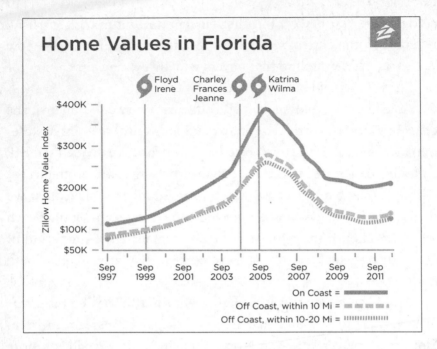

Home Values in Florida

Floyd / Irene · Charley / Frances / Jeanne · Katrina / Wilma

Zillow Home Value Index

$400K · $300K · $200K · $100K · $50K

Sep 1997 · Sep 1999 · Sep 2001 · Sep 2003 · Sep 2005 · Sep 2007 · Sep 2009 · Sep 2011

On Coast =
Off Coast, within 10 Mi =
Off Coast, within 10-20 Mi =

of the housing bubble far better than those in non-coastal areas. In fact, coastal regions have actually appreciated *faster* than non-coastal regions during the past ten years.

WHEN THE MARKET FAILS, THE GOVERNMENT BAILS

It's not surprising that buyers will pay a premium to live on or near the water. It is surprising, however, that the risk of doing so isn't better reflected in housing prices. For economists, that's a red flag that something is distorting the market. And more often than not, that "something" is government policy.

In the case of the coastal housing market, prices are clearly being propped up by the federal government, which has a long history of bailing out homeowners whose properties have been destroyed by tropical storms and hurricanes. Many homes in disaster-prone areas have been rebuilt again and again by government agencies.

It goes without saying that this is bad for Uncle Sam, but in the long run, it's also bad for the housing market and consumers, too.

How did government bailouts become the status quo? It all comes down to the fact that flood insurance is an area where the private market simply doesn't work. It never has.

Here's the problem: If a company sells flood insurance, it might, over time, collect enough premiums to pay out regular claims. But unlike with most other forms of insurance, it takes just one exceptional, devastating event to wipe out all of that accumulated capital. In contrast to health or automobile insurance, which are predicated on the principle that not everyone gets sick or in a car crash at the same moment, flood insurers run the risk of running out of cash in the wake of a big storm. And if they go belly-up, customers will be left holding the bag.

That certainly explains what happened after Hurricane Betsy. When that devastating storm hit the Gulf Coast in September 1965, Congress passed the Southeast Hurricane Disaster Relief Act. This emergency measure bailed out homeowners who could not purchase insurance to protect their homes because, as President Lyndon Johnson said upon signing the bill, "insurance for this type of risk was not available for them to buy."[3]

After Hurricane Betsy, Congress decided it was a good idea to prevent the need for similar bailouts in the future. That's how the National Flood Insurance Program (NFIP) was born, and its purpose was to essentially fill the gap where the private market was not operating.

But the NFIP faces the same issues that the private market would, especially today, as flood-induced catastrophes are increasingly common. For instance, between 1969 and 2005, the NFIP received $7.6 billion more in premiums than in claims. In 2007 and 2008, the NFIP received $3.4 billion more in premiums than in claims.

Yet the program is drowning in debt. Why?

Well, to come full circle, we have two words for you: Hurricane. Katrina.

Katrina, alone, forced the NFIP to pay $16.27 *billion* in claims, which meant that the program had to borrow more than $20 billion from the federal government. This isn't just because the storm caused

Large Flood Insurance Claims

Storm	Year	# Paid Losses	Amount Paid	Average Paid Loss
Hurricane Katrina	Aug 2005	167,722	$16,273,634,517	$97,027
Hurricane Sandy	Oct 2012	63,723	$2,649,099,182	$41,572
Hurricane Ike	Sep 2008	46,418	$2,664,781,987	$57,408
Hurricane Irene	Aug 2011	43,856	$1,303,527,799	$29,723
Tropical Storm Allison	Jun 2001	30,663	$1,103,877,235	$36,000
Hurricane Ivan	Sep 2004	27,658	$1,590,436,206	$57,504
Hurricane Floyd	Sep 1999	20,437	$462,252,753	$22,618
Hurricane Isabel	Sep 2003	19,869	$493,452,308	$24,835
Hurricane Irene	Oct 1999	13,682	$117,858,779	$8,614
Tropical Storm Isaac	Aug 2012	11,287	$487,738,772	$43,212
2010 Nor'easter	Mar 2010	10,087	$194,673,243	$19,299

Source: FEMA, 2013

unprecedented, unforeseen damage. It's also because not enough people participate in the NFIP—even people who live in flood-prone areas.

There are several reasons for the NFIP's low market penetration. Some people just don't understand, and internalize the risk. And in fairness, there's also incomplete information out there about the risk itself. Sometimes, homeowners simply don't know that they live in flood zones. Other times, they rely on levies that end up failing. Some can't afford the premiums. There's also a moral hazard that results from the government coming in and paying for big losses after a disaster. Why buy flood insurance if you know that the government will bail you out anyway?

To address the deficiencies of the NFIP, the government changed the law in 1994. Now federally regulated mortgage lenders are penalized if they don't require flood insurance for properties bought or developed in Special Flood Hazard Areas (SFHAs). And in order to get more folks to purchase flood insurance, the government subsidizes the premiums.

Of course, this has led to another moral hazard. Some people consider this new and improved NFIP as a reason to continue building and rebuilding homes in high-risk areas, creating what are called "severe repetitive loss properties." These are properties that have had multiple NFIP claim payments within a ten-year period. They account for 1 percent of all insured properties—but, alarmingly, up to 30 percent of flood claims.

Put another way, these homes are being rebuilt over and over again, all at taxpayer expense. These frequently flooded homes are a fantastic investment, largely thanks to the largesse of Uncle Sam.

Don't misunderstand us. It is, of course, the collective's obligation to provide assistance to people suffering from disaster damage. We have a responsibility to help our neighbors during times of need. But the purpose of the NFIP was to prevent the need for the federal government to continue doling out billions of dollars in emergency assistance—filling the insurance gap—after every single storm. The program is only effective if people actually buy into it, and if we stop incentivizing the rebuilding of homes in areas that continue suffering catastrophic damage.

This was why, in 2004, the government created a grant program to help acquire, demolish, relocate, elevate, or otherwise flood-proof these properties. In 2012, another, more significant reform was passed to raise the program's premiums to reflect the true risk, making it more expensive to live in those dangerous areas.

Unfortunately, in 2014, Washington took a giant step backward, passing a new round of legislation that repealed or delayed many of its 2012 reforms. What happened there? It was a classic case of concentrated benefits and diffuse costs. Some 1.1 million heavily subsidized, flood-insurance policyholders cried havoc and demanded the restoration of their benefits. The rest of us, meanwhile, hardly noticed—in spite of the fact that we, the taxpayers, are the ones who will foot the bill.

In 1967, not long after Hurricane Betsy devastated New Orleans, Bob Dylan sang, *"If you go down in the flood/It's gonna be your own fault."* Alas, nearly a half-century later, the NFIP is still ensuring that regardless of who's at fault, waterfront property owners will still get their bailouts. It makes for good politics, perhaps. But it's very bad policy.

TWO CURIOUS NOTES REGARDING DISASTERS AND REAL ESTATE

Housing Prices Post-Katrina

Hurricane Katrina was the worst storm in US history, and the New Orleans real estate market's performance in the wake of the storm gives us important insight into the rules that govern coastal property values before and after major disasters.

Before the storm, the average home price in these surviving New Orleans neighborhoods was $203,000. By February 2006, six months after Katrina, the average home price in these affected neighborhoods *jumped* to $222,000.

How can we explain this? After all, the storm displaced huge swaths of the city's population, meaning there were fewer potential home buyers in the months following Katrina. Lower demand should result in lower prices, right?

Yes, but only if the supply remains the same. And after Katrina, there were far fewer properties to buy. The hurricane and flooding destroyed almost 140,000 homes—38 percent of existing housing—in the two most affected parishes, Jefferson and Orleans. And given the extent of the devastation, even though there were fewer people living in the city post-Katrina, there weren't enough homes on the market to meet demand. Among the remaining housing stock, the most desirable properties were snatched up quickly. In other words, at least initially, this was a classic case of increased demand and diminished supply leading to rising prices.

So, what happened after the spike? A drop. By February 2007, the average housing price declined to $197,000 from the pre-Katrina median of $203,000. At that point, only 60 percent of the original population remained in New Orleans. The best, safest housing had already been purchased, leaving behind homes few people wanted. So in the parlance of economists, supply and demand slid back into balance.

Research in the *Journal of Real Estate Finance and Economics* also shows how, after Katrina, buyers in New Orleans were willing to pay a premium for protection against floodwaters, especially in neighborhoods that systematically suffer damage. For instance, before 2005, each additional foot of elevation was valued at 1.4 percent of the home's value. After Katrina—when homes in low-lying areas flooded—the value of extra height jumped up to 4.6 percent per foot.[4]

Havens from Hazards

Here's some advice for the risk adverse: If you want to live far away from natural disasters like wildfires, earthquakes, tornados, and hurricanes like Katrina, check out the list below. We found the ten most populous cities that were farthest from storm tracks and flood plains. Some of these cities are even near the beach! You might consider Michigan's beautiful (albeit frigid) Upper Peninsula, or Oregon's majestic (and usually cloudy) coast.

(NB: Oregon is surrounded by volcanoes...just sayin'.)

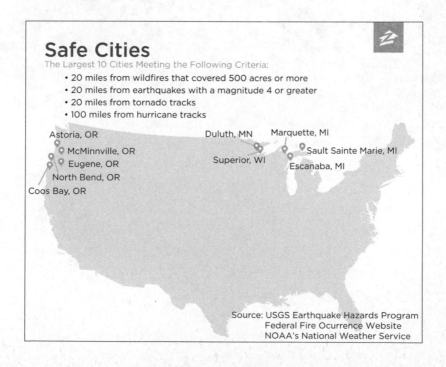

Safe Cities
The Largest 10 Cities Meeting the Following Criteria:
- 20 miles from wildfires that covered 500 acres or more
- 20 miles from earthquakes with a magnitude 4 or greater
- 20 miles from tornado tracks
- 100 miles from hurricane tracks

Astoria, OR
McMinnville, OR
Eugene, OR
North Bend, OR
Coos Bay, OR
Duluth, MN
Marquette, MI
Superior, WI
Sault Sainte Marie, MI
Escanaba, MI

Source: USGS Earthquake Hazards Program
Federal Fire Ocurrence Website
NOAA's National Weather Service

Exterior of the Cleaver family home from the TV show *Leave It to Beaver* (*Photofest*)

Follow the Data to Find Your Way Home

In each of these chapters, we have sought to equip you with the information you need to make better decisions about buying, selling, and renting real estate in the future. Yet one thing we have very consciously *not* done in these pages is hazard a guess about exactly what that future will look like. And this is because the real "dismal science" is not the field of economics, but the field of prediction.

History provides countless examples of humankind's foolhardy prophecies: The 1870s telegraph-company executive who argued, "[the] telephone has too many shortcomings to be seriously considered as a means of communication."[1] The 1920s investors who said radio "has no imaginable commercial value" and inquired, "who would pay for a message sent to nobody in particular?"[2] The 1970s technology executive who could see "no reason anyone would want a computer in their home."[3]

Our point is, people get things wrong all the time. Nobody can foretell precisely what tomorrow holds; there are just too many variables interacting in complicated ways we cannot anticipate. As former US Defense Secretary Donald Rumsfeld famously put it— yes, we're quoting him—"There are known knowns...there are known unknowns...But there are also unknown unknowns."[4] And this especially is true when it comes to America's housing market during a period of recovery and reinvention—as it rebounds from the worst shock, arguably, in its history.

We're all about transparency. Increasing it. Promoting it. Helping consumers to harness its powers to make choices based on information, not hunches. Unfortunately, transparency is different from clairvoyance.

We'd love to end this book with some simple, single sentence of advice such as, "It's time to buy again, but only on Tuesdays!" (And, in fact, that might even be true in some places.) But all we can say with certainty about the housing market's future—the only *known* known—is that we're in for continued volatility. And that volatility will manifest itself differently depending where you are.

It took real estate's hapless, unexamined home value–appreciation machine decades to wind up. Clearly, it's not going to unwind overnight.

We all know the good news: The plane is not going down. Our systems are functioning more efficiently, reliably, and transparently than they were a few years ago. The worst of the turbulence is behind us.

Nevertheless, for the remainder of this decade—and probably into the next—you may be in for a wild ride. So fasten your seat belts. We may experience a few pockets of rough air.

In some places, like the Wild West, for instance, you'll probably see another correction fueled by insanely high appreciation rates after markets have reached bottom. As we showed in Chapter 21, 20-something percent appreciation, year over year, is not a sustainable pace of growth.

In other places, and across the body of America's housing stock as a whole, you'll probably see lower, slower appreciation—the kind of "new normal" that we're watching settle in across our country's economy.

And while we're still seeing some of it now, it's unlikely that we'll witness another era of unchecked, unquestioned, take-it-to-the-bank growth—but not necessarily for the reasons you might expect.

In the aftermath of the housing bubble's rupture, new homes have remained very affordable for people with the financial where-withal to buy. In many places—and in the aggregate—the recent past has been a good time to purchase a home, even as interest rates inch back up from their record lows.

WARNING SIGNS OF A BUBBLE

Nevertheless, in a number of metro areas, homes yet again are becoming more *unaffordable* than ever. They make up a new hous-ing bubble—a bubble that has swelled as a direct consequence of the last one's explosion. And this bubble is artificially inflated by two forces of distortion: lots of negative equity and low mortgage rates.

How does this work? Let's take these factors one at a time.

■ **Watch negative equity.** Negative equity constrains the hous-ing supply because potential sellers—who would have to pay the difference in cash if their home is worth less than the mortgage balance—avoid becoming actual sellers. The data tells us that, not long ago, nearly half of Americans with a mortgage lacked suffi-cient equity to sell their current home and then make a down pay-ment on another one. These homeowners are underwater—and the housing market is undersupplied as a result.

■ **Are mortgage rates driving up demand?** Low mortgage rates drive up demand. The less expensive it is to finance a home pur-chase, the more likely it is that folks who are thinking of buying will be able to go ahead and do so. And, of course, when high demand meets limited supply, prices go up—and the bubble just keeps on expanding.

These higher prices are creating affordability issues below the water line—issues that can't be solved while mortgage rates are so low. And yet, as interest rates continue rising, then, sure as death and taxes, all this is going to change. Why? Because, as rates increase, potential buyers will be less eager, removing demand from the marketplace and halting appreciation in its tracks. In other words, a spike in interest rates will actually reduce the threat of a bubble.

And so, as we said, the worst is behind us. But that doesn't mean the next decade will be either smooth or simple.

Regardless of which ZIP code you call home, you may be asking, "What does this mean for *my* major, life-altering financial decision?"

The answer is simple: Let the data be your guide. Precisely because it is harder than ever to make accurate predictions about the future—just think about all those *unknown* unknowns out there—it's more important than ever to make the best-informed possible decisions you can today. This means navigating by the numbers, not only by your intuition.

This is especially crucial when addressing a pair of questions on the minds of a lot of Americans nowadays: "Is it safe for me to get back in the housing market?" And "Can we prevent another meltdown like the one from which Americans are just beginning to recover?"

We believe the answer to both questions is "yes." But this is not because the days of instability and uncertainty in the housing market are over. Quite simply, they're not. Rather, we believe that now is a safe time to sell or buy because volatility's mere existence simply doesn't matter as much today as it did five years ago.

In the new realm of real estate, everyone faces a rather stark choice. The operative question now is: Do you wield the power of data to your advantage? Or do you ignore the data, to your peril?

The same is true of the housing market writ large. Certainly, many macro-level dynamics are out of any one person's control. And yet, we're better equipped than ever before to choose wisely in the present—to make the kinds of measured judgments that can prevent another coast-to-coast bubble and calamitous burst.

On the individual level, this means heeding the wisdom of the numbers—in determining where you buy and when you sell; the kind of mortgage terms to which you agree and how many words you include in your listing. These are small actions that add up to a big difference. They can help you make the right moves in spite of the fact that you're navigating uncertain terrain.

On the macro level, the data allows policy makers to understand and channel the forces and factors at play in our wider real estate market—to prevent them from upending our economy as they did so dramatically just a few years ago.

Now that we all can access the data, we don't need to feel lost, or helpless, or hopeless. We're not flying blind anymore. Where we used to be feeling out our way in the dark, we've now flipped on the light switch. There's much to see that can help us make smarter choices—as consumers, as policy makers, as a community.

Yes, some sub-markets will continue to have hiccups. No, your house is not a guaranteed money factory.

But if you're smart and savvy, if you sell wisely and buy cautiously, then there are deals to be had—and there's no reason you can't find them and make them yours.

Which brings us to the most important new rule of real estate among them all: Get your hands on as much information as you can. Recognize that you're buying and selling in a local market, not a national one, and learn as much as you can about it.

Follow wherever the data leads you. Let the zillions help you rest more easily. Numbers don't lie. And they won't lead you astray. Indeed, they'll help you find your way home.

A NOTE ON OUR METHODOLOGY

At the core of this book is Zillow's unprecedented real estate data, which sheds light on all of the topics we've tackled here. It also serves to inform better, smarter decisions by people, investors, and policy makers alike. Moreover, Zillow's tens of millions of users every month, trying to make sense of the new world order of housing, provide an ever-sharpening, often surprising picture of America's behavior in, preferences for, and desires about the places we live. We thank them and hope they keep coming.

Our database of homes is a living, breathing entity. It's alive, in one sense, because it's constantly updated and improved. Today, more than 50 million homes—just fewer than half of all homes in the United States—have been updated on Zillow by their owners or the owner's real estate agent. Our community—including, we imagine, many of you who read this book—connect with us multiple times a week, if not multiple times a day. But our database is also a living thing in another sense: The ways, places, and times that people use it—in the aggregate—reveal powerful trends in the housing market.

What makes our database unique is more than the frequency with which it's accessed and updated, and more than its sheer size. Sure, it's pretty cool that our database includes practically every address in America—then again, the phone book laid claim to that distinction long before Zillow was a twinkle in the Internet's eye. Rather, our differentiating factor is that we have a database not just of all homes, but of all *home values*—going back for decades. By adding the dimension of time, we can analyze our data for developments that have powerful implications about how the housing market is performing today, and how it is likely to perform in the future.

We owe an intellectual debt to some influential researchers, some of whom we call out in the text, and others, who are more unsung heroes, in the endnotes that follow.

Any errors of omission (or commission) are ours, and ours alone.

—*Stan and Spencer*

ACKNOWLEDGMENTS

As with any endeavor of this size, there are lots and lots of people who helped make this book a reality.

First, we want to thank our tireless research assistant, Meredith Miller, who helped shepherd, cajole, and corral all the many details that went into the long research and writing process, and our extraordinary writing partners Jonas Kieffer and Ben Yarrow, who were ably assisted by Zev Karlin-Neumann, Clare Doody, Mike Flynn, and the team at West Wing Writers. This group was our constant companions throughout this process, and we could not have asked for a merrier or more capable band of compatriots.

The talented Zillow Economics team, led by Dr. Svenja Gudell, fueled most of the analysis contained in these pages. Dr. Skylar Olsen contributed to many of the key book chapters along with Dr. Krishna Rao, Matthew Fix, Clark Lundberg, Austin Gross, Nalina Varanasi, Laine Rutledge, and Yi-An Chen. At Zillow, we want to approach real estate issues with creativity, insight, and methodological rigor, and all three of these traits were abundantly present in the countless hours of research and iteration that went into this book.

Many other Zillowites helped along the way, especially Amy Bohutinsky, who was essentially our third partner in the overall effort, and many folks who read and commented on numerous drafts, including Kathleen Phillips, Diane Tuman, and Mitch Robinson. Sarah Makar was instrumental in our cover design and graphic art, and Alessandra Arendt helped out with many of the images. Jeanne Brennan and Heather Dunning helped us to somehow find the time in our schedules to work on this project, a feat that is perhaps the biggest one of all.

We were also fortunate in this project to get to work with dozens of smart people outside of Zillow who helped enrich our data, insights, and stories, including Josh Herst and Matt Lerner from Walk Score; Arthur Rubinfeld, Patrick O'Hagan, Dave West, and Brendan O'Shaughnessy from Starbucks headquarters; Dr. Thomas Thibodeau from the University of Colorado, Boulder; Joe Cortright from Impresa, Inc.; Chuck Eberl and Susan Frankel from Healthways, and the Gallup team working on the Gallup-Healthways Well-Being Index. We also appreciate the assistance of the Interuniversity Consortium for Political and Social Research at the University of Michigan for access to data from the General Social Survey.

We appreciate the help of Kinney Zalesne with the initial book proposal and thinking through early concepts for what this book would become.

We want to especially thank our agent, Jennifer Joel at ICM Partners, who helped two neophytes navigate the world of publishing, which turns out to be quite different than the Internet world (to put it mildly), and John Brodie, our original editor at Grand Central Publishing, who initially spurred us into action, was always a font of enthusiasm, and helped us find the right vision for this book from among the many competing visions we could have adopted. We would also like to thank Rick Wolff and his colleague Dan Berkowitz for their work. Finally, thanks to Ben Greenberg, Yasmin Mathew, and Maddie Caldwell at Grand Central, who helped us across the finish line.

Finally, we want to thank Rich Barton and Lloyd Frink, without whom Zillow would not exist, for their support and guidance through the years.

As is always the case, these people only helped us, and any errors or missteps herein are entirely our own.

If not stated otherwise, the data used in images belongs to Zillow.

Introduction: Leaving Home

1. Geoffrey Brewer, "Snakes Top List of Americans' Fears," Gallup News Service (March 19, 2001), http://www.gallup.com/poll/1891/snakes-top-list-americans -fears.aspx.

2. William Safire, "Location, Location, Location," *New York Times* (June 26, 2009), http://www.nytimes.com/2009/06/28/magazine/28FOB-onlanguage-t.html.

3. Alex Wilson and Jessica Boehland, "Small is Beautiful, U.S. House Size, Resource Use and the Environment", *Journal of Industrial Economy*, 9, no.1-2 (2008), http://onlinelibrary.wiley.com/doi/10.1162/1088198054084680/pdf.

Chapter 1: Warren Buffett Is (Always) Right

1. "The World's Billionaires," *Forbes*, http://www.forbes.com/profile/ warren-buffett/.

2. "Berkshire's Corporate Performance vs. the S&P 500," http://www.berkshire hathaway.com/letters/2012ltr.pdf.

3. "Warren Buffett Watch: Keeping Track of America's Billionaire Next Door," CNBC.com (February 27, 2012), http://fm.cnbc.com/applications/cnbc .com/resources/editorialfiles/2012/07/03/2012-02-27%20Ask%20Warren%20 Transcript.pdf.

4. Ibid.

5. "Home Sweet Home. Still," Pew Research Social & Demographic Trends (April 12, 2011), http://www.pewsocialtrends.org/2011/04/12/home-sweet-home-still.

6. "National Housing Survey Monthly Indicators," Fannie Mae (May 2014), http://www.fanniemae.com/portal/research-and-analysis/housing-monthly.html.

7. The World Bank, "Data: Market Capitalization of Listed Countries (Current US$)," http://data.worldbank.org/indicator/CM.MKT.LCAP.CD.

Chapter 2: Stats and the City

1. Zillow listing, http://www.zillow.com/homes/64-perry-street-west-village ,-new-york_rb/#/homedetails/64-Perry-St-New-York-NY-10014/31500839_zpid/.

2. Ibid.

3. Caroline Kim, " 'Sex and the City' Townhouse Sold for $9.85 Million," Yahoo! Finance (April 25, 2012), http://finance.yahoo.com/blogs/the-exchange/sex -city-townhouse-sold-9-85-million-180215800.html.

Chapter 4: The Starbucks Effect

1. "Starbucks Company Profile" (January 2014), Starbucks.com, http:// globalassets.starbucks.com/assets/e12a69d0d51e45d58567ea9fc433ca1f.pdf.
2. "Most-Shocking-Starbucks-Locations," Jaunted, http://www.jaunted.com/ maps/Most-Shocking-Starbucks-Locations.
3. "Starbucks Company Profile" (January 2014), Starbucks.com, http:// globalassets.starbucks.com/assets/e12a69d0d51e45d58567ea9fc433ca1f.pdf.

Chapter 5: It's the Worst House for a Reason

1. Ellen Rand, "New Jersey Housing: From Rags to Riches in Monmouth," *New York Times* (September 30, 1979).
2. This Old House, http://www.thisoldhouse.com/toh/photos/0,20392272 _20795989,00.html.
3. Cheryl Lavin, "Fast Track. Replays: 'Always be a little kinder than necessary.' – James...," *Chicago Tribune* (October 13, 1996), http://articles.chicago tribune.com/1996-10-13/features/9610130394_1_drunk-liar-ugliest-house.
4. Ibid.
5. Lynn Harris, "Park Slope: Where Is the Love?," *New York Times* (May 18, 2008), http://www.nytimes.com/2008/05/18/fashion/18slope.html?pagewanted=all.
6. "Renovations Continue in Manchester Neighborhood," CBS Pittsburgh (July 20, 2011), http://pittsburgh.cbslocal.com/2011/07/20/renovations-continue -in-manchester-neighborhood/.

Chapter 6: Do Your Homework

1. Sam DeBord, "The Right School District: How Much Do Schools Affect Real Estate Prices?," Realtor.com (August 21, 2013), http://www.realtor.com /advice/the-right-school-district-how-much-do-schools-affect-real-estate-prices/.
2. "The GreatSchools Rating," GreatSchools.org, http://www.greatschools .org/find-a-school/defining-your-ideal/2423-ratings.gs#1.

Chapter 7: ARMs and Legs

1. David Foster Wallace, "Tense Present," *Harper's Magazine* (April 2001).
2. Ibid.
3. "Faith in Flux", Pew Research Religion & Public Life Project (April 27, 2009), http://www.pewforum.org/2009/04/27/faith-in-flux//.
4. "Employee Tenure Summary," Bureau of Labor Statistics (September 2014), http://www.bls.gov/news.release/tenure.nr0.htm.

5. "Number, Timing and Duration of Marriages and Divorces: 2009", U.S. Census Bureau (2011), https://www.census.gov/prod/2011pubs/p70-125.pdf.

6. *Merriam-Webster Dictionary*, s.v. "mortgage," http://www.merriam-webster.com/dictionary/mortgage.

7. Ann-Margret Westin et al., "Global Financial Stability Report: Durable Financial Stability: Getting There from Here," *International Monetary Fund* (April 2011), 16, http://www.imf.org/external/pubs/ft/gfsr/2011/01/pdf/chap3.pdf.

8. Wallace, 95.

Chapter 10: America's Next Top Remodel

1. "Measuring the Benefits of Home Remodeling," Joint Center for Housing Studies of Harvard University (September 8, 2003), http://www.jchs.harvard.edu/research/publications/measuring-benefits-home-remodeling.

2. Warmly Yours, blog. http://www.warmlyyours.com/en-US/posts/lava-panels—Home-Improvement-Spending-Rises-in-2013-Trends-Include-Radiant-Heat—926.

Chapter 11: Magic Words and Dangerous Descriptors

1. Amy Webb, "Hacking the Hyperlinked Heart," *Wall Street Journal* (updated January 14, 2013), http://online.wsj.com/article/SB100014241278873233745045782 17973101313736.html#printMode.

2. Steven D. Levitt and Stephen J. Dubner, *Freakonomics: A Rogue Economist Explores the Hidden Side of Everything* (New York: Harper Perennial, 2009), 75.

Chapter 14: Real Est8 4 Sale

1. John Roach, "Friday the 13th Phobia Rooted in Ancient History," *National Geographic News* (updated August 12, 2004), http://news.nationalgeographic.com/news/2004/02/0212_040212_friday13.html.

Chapter 16: Nine Is the Magic Number

1. Shan Lee, "Dave Gold Dies at 80; Entrepreneur Behind 99¢ Only Chain," *Los Angeles Times* (April 26, 2013), http://www.latimes.com/news/obituaries/la-me-dave-gold-20130427,0,3173330.story.

2. Tim Arango, "Bet Your Bottom Dollar on 99 Cents," *New York Times* (February 7, 2009), http://www.nytimes.com/2009/02/08/weekinreview/08arango.html.

3. Robert M. Schindler and Thomas M. Kibarian, "Increased Consumer Sales Response through Use of 99 Ending Prices," *Journal of Retailing* 72, no. 2 (1996), http://camden-sbc.rutgers.edu/facultystaff/research/schindler/Schindler%20%26%20Kibarian%20(1996).pdf.

4. William Poundstone, *Priceless: The Myth of Fair Value and How to Take Advantage of It* (New York: Hill and Wang, 2011), 188-9.

Chapter 17: Appraising Real Estate Agents

1. Reece Realty, http://www.reecerealty.com/advertize/7-1-08.pdf.
2. Melissa Dittmann Tracey, "Can a Catchy Slogan Make You Stand Out?," *RealtorMag* (May 2012), http://realtormag.realtor.org/sales-and-marketing/feature/article/2012/05/can-catchy-slogan-make-you-stand-out.
3. Realty Executives, http://barbnickels.realtyx.com/contact/index.php?aid =000100707&temp=1058&aname=Barb+and+Jim+Nickels&aimg=1&agent _hasfeat=6&.
4. "Profile of Home Buyers and Sellers 2012," National Association of REALTORS®.
5. Joseph Stiglitz, "Of the 1%, by the 1%, for the 1%", *Vanity Fair* (May 2011), http://www.vanityfair.com/society/features/2011/05/top-one-percent-201105.

Chapter 18: The Gayborhood Phenomenon

1. Prashant Gopal, "Ohio Study Shows Varying Role of Gay Couples in Property Values," *Bloomberg BusinessWeek* (November 7, 2011), http://www.businessweek.com/news/2011-11-07/ohio-study-shows-varying-role-of-gay-couples-in-property-values.html.
2. Patricia Leigh Brown, "Gay Enclaves Face Prospect of Being Passé," *New York Times* (October 30, 2007), http://www.nytimes.com/2007/10/30/us/30gay.html.
3. "Changing Attitudes on Gay Marriage," Pew Research Religion & Public Life Project (March 10, 2014), http://features.pewforum.org/same-sex-marriage-attitudes/index.php.

Chapter 19: What's in a Street Name?

1. The Virginia Room, "Do You Know What Your Street Name Used to Be?," Arlington Public Library, "In Our Back Pages" (January 15, 2013), http://library.arlingtonva.us/2013/01/15/do-you-know-what-your-street-used-to-be-named-back-pages/.

Chapter 20: Empire Real Estate of Mind

1. Lyrics Freak, Rolling Stones, "Shattered" lyrics, http://www.lyricsfreak.com/r/rolling+stones/shattered_20117877.html.
2. "New York: A City of Neighborhoods," New York City Planning, http://www.nyc.gov/html/dcp/html/neighbor/neigh.shtml.
3. Zillow listing, http://www.zillow.com/homedetails/102-Avenue-B-APT-4-New-York-NY-10009/79493758_zpid/ and Zillow listing, http://www.zillow.com/homedetails/506-E-6th-St-4-New-York-NY-10009/2114342587_zpid/.
4. United States Census Bureau, http://quickfacts.census.gov/qfd/states/36/3651000.html.

5. "U.S. Census Bureau: State and County QuickFacts," American Community Survey.

6. Mitchell Hall, "Manhattan Residential Architecture," nyc BLOG estate (May 17, 2011), http://nycblogestate.com/2007/05/manhattan-residential-architecture.html.

7. Christopher Gray, "An Innovation Packed with Artists," *New York Times* (April 4, 2013), http://www.nytimes.com/2013/04/07/realestate/the-idea-behind-the -co-op-building.html.

8. Susan Stellin, "Co-op Vs. Condo: The Differences Are Narrowing," *New York Times* (October 5, 2012), http://www.nytimes.com/2012/10/07/realestate/ getting-started-choosing-between-a-co-op-and-a-condo.html?pagewanted=all.

9. Zillow listing, http://www.zillow.com/homedetails/8-Spruce-St-New-York -NY-10038/2118419674_zpid/.

10. Julie Satow, "Looking Down on the Empire State," *New York Times* (June 7, 2013), http://www.nytimes.com/2013/06/09/realestate/new-york-citys-skyscraper -war.html.

11. Spike Lee, "Spike Lee's Open Letter to the New York Times," *WhoSay* (March 31, 2014), http://www.whosay.com/articles/1557-spike-lees-open-letter-to -the-new-york-times.

12. José Acosta, trans. Emily Leavitt, "Thousands Forced to Leave Upper Manhattan," *Voices of NY* (February 28, 2013), http://www.voicesofny.org/2013/ 02/thousands-forced-to-leave-upper-manhattan/.

13. Mireya Navarro, "Tenants Living Amid Rubble in Rent-Regulated Apart-ment War," *New York Times* (February 24, 2014), http://www.nytimes.com/ 2014/02/25/nyregion/in-new-york-push-for-market-rate-housing-pits-landlords -against-tenants.html.

14. "Russian Buyers Hunt Trophy Properties in NYC and Beyond," *The Real Deal* (August 3, 2011), http://therealdeal.com/blog/2011/08/03/russian-buyers -hunt-trophy-properties-in-nyc-and-beyond/.

15. Morgan Brennan, "Real Estate Tourism: Who's Really Buying America's Homes?," *Forbes* (August 10, 2012), http://www.forbes.com/sites/morganbrennan/ 2012/08/10/real-estate-tourism-whos-really-buying-americas-homes/.

16. James Orr and Georgio Topa, "Challenges Facing the New York Metropoli-tan Area Economy," *Current Issues in Economics and Finance, Second District High-lights, Federal Reserve Bank of New York*, 12, no. 2 (1996), http://www.newyorkfed .org/research/current_issues/ci12-1.pdf.

17. Patrick McGeehan, "Income Soars on Wall Street, Widening Gap," *New York Times* (November 23, 2006), http://www.nytimes.com/2006/11/23/nyregion/ 23income.html?ref=nyregion.

18. Jennifer Parker, "Post 9/11, Wall Street Goes from Rubble to Renaissance," *USA Today* (updated September 2, 2011), http://usatoday30.usatoday.com/money/economy/ story/2011-09-04/Post-911-Wall-Street-goes-from-rubble-to-renaissance/50245410/1.

19. The World Factbook, Central Intelligence Agency Library, https://www
.cia.gov/library/publications/the-world-factbook/rankorder/2172rank.html.

20. Simon Kuper, "International Cities Are Turning Into 'Elite Citadels,'"
Business Insider (June 17, 2013), http://www.businessinsider.com/global-cities-too
-expensive-paris-2013-6.

Chapter 21: The Wild, Wild West

1. Barry Wood, "Stuck in Phoenix, the Epicenter of Housing Crisis," *Yahoo!*
Finance (July 28, 2011), http://finance.yahoo.com/news/pf_article_113212.html.

2. Ibid.

3. Kevin Anderson, "US Elections: A Housing Crisis Tour of Riverside," *DeadlineUSA Blog* (October 10, 2008), http://www.guardian.co.uk/world/
deadlineusa/2008/oct/10/uselections2008-useconomy.

4. Associated Press, "Vegas Called Least Educated, Most Economically Volatile
City in West," RGJ.com (January 7, 2011), http://archive.rgj.com/viewart/20110107/
NEWS/110107014/Vegas-called-least-educated-most-economically-volatile-city-West.

Chapter 23: What's Walkability Worth?

1. Alex Williams, "Creating Hipsturbia," *New York Times* (February 15, 2013),
http://www.nytimes.com/2013/02/17/fashion/creating-hipsturbia-in-the-suburbs
-of-new-york.html?pagewanted=all&_r=0.

2. Kristen Wyatt, "Young Adults Choose Cities Over Suburban Living as
'Generation Rent' Faces Tough Economy," *HuffPost Business* (June 28, 2012,
updated: November 16, 2012), http://www.huffingtonpost.com/2012/06/28/young
-adults-cities-generation-rent_n_1632952.html?view=print&comm_ref=false.

Chapter 24: Owning Isn't for Everyone

1. "President Calls for Expanding Opportunities to Home Ownership," The
White House: President W. George Bush (press release) (June 17, 2002), http://
georgewbush-whitehouse.archives.gov/news/releases/2002/06/20020617-2.html.

2. Barbara Kiviat, "The Case Against Homeownership," *Time* (September 11,
2010), http://content.time.com/time/magazine/article/0,9171,2013850,00.html.

3. William J. Clinton, "Remarks on the National Homeownership Strategy,"
The American Presidency Project (June 5, 1995), http://www.presidency.ucsb.edu/
ws/?pid=51448.

4. "Reaching the Dream—Atlanta," U. S. Department of Housing and Urban
Development, "Archives" (June 23, 2010), http://archives.hud.gov/initiatives/fbci/
dream/atlanta.cfm.

5. Jo Becker, Sheryl Gay Stolberg, and Stephen Labaton, "Bush Drive for Home
Ownership Fueled Housing Bubble," *New York Times* (December 21, 2008), http://
www.nytimes.com/2008/12/21/business/worldbusiness/21iht-admin.4.18853088
.html?pagewanted=all.

6.   Ibid.

7.   Annie Lowrey, "Income Inequality May Take Toll on Growth," *New York Times* (October 16, 2012), http://www.nytimes.com/2012/10/17/business/economy/income-inequality-may-take-toll-on-growth.html?pagewanted=all.

Chapter 25: The Third Rail of Real Estate

1.   Dennis J. Ventry Jr., "The Accidental Deduction: A History and Critique of the Tax Subsidy for Mortgage Interest," *Law and Contemporary Problems* 73, no. 233, http://scholarship.law.duke.edu/cgi/viewcontent.cgi?article=1561&context=lcp.

2.   http://www.va.gov/budget/docs/summary/Fy2013_Fast_Facts_VAs_Budget_Highlights.pdf.

3.   Mattea Kramer, "You Ask We Answer: How Much Does the U.S. Spend on Foreign Aid," National Priorities Project (October 22, 2012), http://nationalpriorities.org/blog/2012/10/22/you-ask-we-answer-how-much-does-us-spend-foreign-aid/.

4.   "Policy Basics: Introduction to the Supplemental Nutrition Assistance Program (SNAP)," Center on Budget and Policy Priorities (updated: June 4, 2014), http://www.centeronbudget.org/cms/index.cfm?fa=view&id=2226.

5.   *Fiscal Year 2013 Analytical Perspectives: Budget of the U.S. Government*, 261, http://www.whitehouse.gov/sites/default/files/omb/budget/fy2013/assets/spec.pdf.

6.   "Realtors® Urge Preserving of Homeownership Tax Policies," National Association of Realtors® (press release) (April 25, 2013), http://www.realtor.org/news-releases/2013/04/realtors-urge-preserving-of-homeownership-tax-policies.

7.   Bruce Ramsay, "Home Ownership in the United States versus Canada," *Seattle Times*, "Editorials/Opinion" (August 12, 2013), http://blogs.seattletimes.com/opinionnw/2013/08/12/homeownership-in-the-united-states-versus-canada/.

8.   Margery Austin Turner, Eric Toder, Rolf Pendal, Claudia Sharygin, "How Would Reforming the Mortgage Interest Deduction Affect the Housing Market?," Urban Institute (March 2013), http://www.taxpolicycenter.org/UploadedPDF/412776-How-Would-Reforming-the-Mortgage-Interest-Deduction-Affect-the-Housing-Market.pdf.

9.   Anthony Randazzo and Dean Stansel, "Unmasking the Mortgage Interest Deduction: Who Benefits and How Much?," Reason Foundation Policy Summary (July 2011), http://reason.org/files/midsummary_final.pdf.

10. Todd Sinai and Joseph Gyourko, "The (Un)Changing Geographical Distribution of Housing Tax Benefits: 1980 to 2000" (abstract: The Wharton School, University of Pennsylvania, November 20, 2003), http://real.wharton.upenn.edu/~sinai/papers/Geog_distribution_112003.pdf.

11. Dan Horn, "Middle Class a Matter of Income, Attitude," *USA Today* (April 14, 2013), http://www.usatoday.com/story/money/business/2013/04/14/middle-class-hard-define/2080565/.

12. Anthony Randazzo, "Study: Time to Eliminate the Mortgage Interest Deduction," Reason Foundation, http://reason.org/news/show/eliminate-mortgage-interest-deducti

Chapter 26: Down by the Seaside

1. Andrew Restuccia, "Report: Climate Change Triggers Extreme Weather Events," *Politico Pro* (January 11, 2013), http://www.politico.com/story/2013/01/report-climate-change-triggers-extreme-weather-events-86067.html#ixzz2U9Ts3wP1.

2. "Summary of Hurricane Irene in Southeast Florida," National Weather Service Weather Forecast Office: Miami–South Florida (January 6, 2009), http://www.srh.noaa.gov/mfl/?n=1999_irene.

3. Lyndon B. Johnson, "605 - Statement by the President Upon Signing the Southeast Hurricane Disaster Relief Act of 1965," The American Presidency Project (November 8, 1965), http://www.presidency.ucsb.edu/ws/?pid=27358.

4. Russell McKenzie and John Levendis, "Flood Hazards and Urban Housing Markets: The Effects of Katrina on New Orleans" (abstract, Southeastern Louisiana University, Loyola University New Orleans, September 29, 2009), Social Science Research Network, http://papers.ssrn.com/sol3/papers.cfm?abstract_id=1480294##.

Conclusion: Follow the Data to Find Your Way Home

1. Charlotte Gray, *Reluctant Genius: Alexander Graham Bell and the Passion for Invention* (New York: Arcade Publishing, 2006), http://books.google.com/books?id=ujlCgf1uSJIC&pg=PA129&lpg=PA129&dq=william+orton+western+union+the+telephone+has+too+many+shortcomings+to+be+seriously+considered+as+a+means+of+communication.%E2%80%9D&source=bl&ots=11jP-_iggs&sig=z4v-nx56nMaSthxPYoTDlqyNrds&hl=en&sa=X&ei=Ppk5U75r1MyxBIbyg JgF&ved=0CEkQ6AEwBA#v=onepage&q&f=false.

2. "The Future of Time Travel," *NOVA* Online, http://www.pbs.org/wgbh/nova/time/through2.html.

3. Erin Skarda, "Top 10 Failed Predictions: Technology, What's That?," *Time* (October 21, 2012), http://content.time.com/time/specials/packages/article/0,28804,2097462_2097456_2097467,00.html.

4. Secretary Rumsfeld and Gen. Myers, "DoD News Briefing," U.S. Department of Defense, http://www.defense.gov/transcripts/transcript.aspx?transcriptid=2636.

INDEX